EVOLUTION

by

FRANK H. T. RHODES
The University of Michigan

ILLUSTRATED BY
REBECCA MERRILEES
and
RUDY ZALLINGER

 GOLDEN PRESS • NEW YORK

Western Publishing Company, Inc.
Racine, Wisconsin

FOREWORD

How life arose and how man developed are two questions that are as old as man himself, as the creation accounts of many civilizations bear witness. But ancient as is this concern, the implications of man's relationship to the world of living things are as significant in the Space Age as they were in the Stone Age. This book is a simple account of man's search for those origins and relationships. It describes the historical development of the present theory of evolution, or descent with modification, the indications that support it, its nature and mechanism, and its result in the long history of life.

The book concludes with a section on the meaning of evolution, for the theory of evolution has had a profound impact on man's view of himself and his relationship to the world in which he lives. Evolutionary theory provides a powerful explanation of how life developed, yet beyond it, and unanswered by it, lies the ultimate question of why life developed. That question, confronting as it does the larger significance of life, though the abstractive methods of science provide no appropriate solution to it, is neither meaningless nor inconsequential. For in our response to it, individually and collectively, lies the future of evolution, and with it the future of mankind.

I am grateful to my colleague Dr. Alfred Smith who kindly read the manuscript of this book.

Frank H. T. Rhodes

CONTENTS

OVERVIEW OF LIFE

Earth teems with life. Living creatures exist from ocean depths to the highest mountain peaks, from equatorial jungles and hot mineral springs to the frozen polar wastelands, from the blinding brightness and aridity of the desert to the dark intestines of animals. In each environment, untold numbers of individual organisms inhabit every nook and cranny of the available space.

Most animal and plant species contain a myriad individuals. Thus the surface layer of most meadow soils contains several million animals per acre. Microscopic animals and plants exist in uncountable numbers. One gram of soil may contain hundreds of millions of living things. Birds and insects exist in populations so vast as to constitute local "plague" conditions. Aquatic life is no less prolific.

It is unlikely that the earth is unique in this respect. It has been calculated that there may be millions of planets in other parts of the universe capable of supporting some form of life.

Each environment supports a distinctive community of plants and animals.

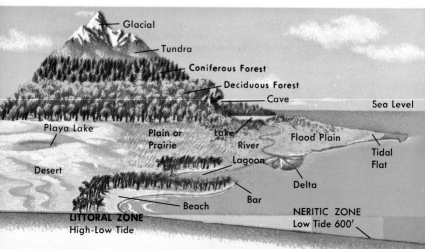

6. Other invertebrates—21,000

5. Wormlike phyla—38,000

4. Protozoans—30,000

3. Chordates—45,000

2. Mollusks—45,000

1. Arthropods—900,000

MAJOR GROUPS (PHYLA)
OF ANIMALS—OVER
1,000,000 SPECIES

DIVERSITY OF LIFE is shown by the existence of more than one million kinds (species) of animals and more than 350,000 kinds of plants.

Animals range in size from a few thousandths of an inch to more than 100 feet in length. They represent a vast variety of ways of life—parasites, predators, herbivores, swimmers, fliers, crawlers, burrowers. Some spend their lives fixed in one spot; others undertake seasonal migrations of thousands of miles.

In spite of the many kinds of animals and plants, they represent only a few basic groups (phyla).

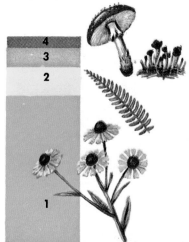

4. Algae and Fungi—60,000

3. Mosses and Liverworts—23,000

2. Ferns, Conifers, etc.—10,000

1. Flowering Plants—250,000

MAJOR GROUPS (PHYLA)
OF PLANTS—ABOUT
350,000 SPECIES

5

THE DEVELOPMENT OF LIFE has always been one of man's great concerns. Ancient sacred writings of many faiths discuss this question. The early chapters of the Book of Genesis, for example, deal with the sequence of creation, and Adam named the different kinds of animals. The need to classify living things was partly practical. Some plants were poisonous, others edible. Some animals were harmful, others were not. Early man's survival depended on his skill in recognizing each kind. Man's daily experience and religious tradition coincided here: every animal and plant that he recognized reproduced "after its own kind."

Man's early life as a hunter brought him in close contact with animals, and ancient cave paintings bear a record of his interest. Later domestication of animals and harvesting of crops increased this concern.

Creation of Adam from Michelangelo's painting of Sistine Chapel Ceiling.

ARISTOTLE, Greek philosopher, was also one of the first and greatest biologists. He wrote extensively on the classification and structure of over 500 species of animals from the Mediterranean area. Aristotle was a gifted observer, and described details of such things as chick embryology. He accepted the spontaneous generation of flies from putrefying matter, but was also concerned about the problems of heredity.

ARISTOTLE (384-322 B. C.), pupil of Plato and tutor of Alexander the Great, observed that species appeared to be unchanging. Cows produced only cows; horses arose only from horses. Between the two there was a clear division. Species were characterized by their reproductive isolation. Individuals developed, according to Aristotle, by the capacity (psyche) of each to conform to the archetype characters of the species relationships. He constructed a "ladder of Nature" showing the unity of plan.

In contrast to Aristotle's "vitalist" views, the Democritans were "mechanists." They believed that an organism's activity was the result of the interaction of the atoms of which it was made. Although vitalistic and mechanistic controversies still persist, the supposed conflict between science and religion being an example, the two views are often complementary, not competitive. In some situations, we need to use both (p. 155). The discussion in this book is mechanistic ("how" things develop, not "why"), but that does not mean that life has no meaning and purpose.

THE ORIGIN OF LIFE was long regarded as a spontaneous event: living things arose from nonliving matter. Although the various groups of living things were believed to have been created in definite sequence, it was supposed that each kind of animal and plant arose "fully formed" from the dust of the earth. Such a view involved no obvious contradictions. Flies, for example, could be seen to develop from maggots, which arose "spontaneously" in decaying meat. The spontaneous generation of living things became a universal assumption. We still speak of dirt "breeding" vermin. The view was also economical: it involved only one category of explanation. Our current popular views require not only an explanation for the origin of life but also one for the origin of species.

Early views on the origin of life included one that suggested sheep arose from a plant. (After Weinberg.)

SPONTANEOUS GENERATION of living creatures from nonliving matter became increasingly suspect in the seventeenth century. Francesco Redi (1621-97), an Italian physician, became convinced that the maggots found in meat were derived not from the meat itself but from eggs laid by flies.

Open—
flies, decaying
meat, and maggots

Closed—
meat decaying,
but no flies or maggots

REDI placed a "dead snake, some fish, and a slice of veal" in four open-mouthed flasks, and then placed the same things in four flasks that he closed and sealed. Flies constantly settled on the meat in the open flasks, which became wormy. No worms appeared on the meat in the sealed flasks.

Knowing that some believed air to be essential for generation, Redi repeated the experiment, this time using a gauze cover for the "closed" flasks to protect them from flies but allowing air inside. Again, no maggots appeared on the meat. This discredited the most familiar example of spontaneous generation.

A REFINED VERSION of Redi's experiment was used by Pasteur in the mid-eighteenth century to demonstrate that putrefaction and fermentation depend on action of air-borne organisms.

Open—
flies and
maggots on
decaying meat

Covered with
gauze—
no flies or
maggots on
decaying meat

9

A CLASSIFICATION OF LIFE was devised by Aristotle in the fourth century B. C. and stood undisputed for nineteen centuries. This classification embraced a complete gradation from the lowest to the highest organism—man.

Fifteenth and sixteenth century voyages of discovery and the invention of the microscope revealed a diversity of animal and plant form and function unknown to Aristotle. With these new observations, changes in classification took place.

JOHN RAY (1627-1705), an English naturalist, introduced the present idea of species and higher categories in classification. Ray showed that groups of similar species could be classified into sets, which he called *genera*. This system is the basis for the international one still being used today.

CARL LINNAEUS (1707-1778), a Swedish naturalist, developed the present system and method of biological classification (taxonomy). He used a uniform system of classification and nomenclature. The 10th edition of his *Systema Naturae* (1758) marks the beginning of modern taxonomy.

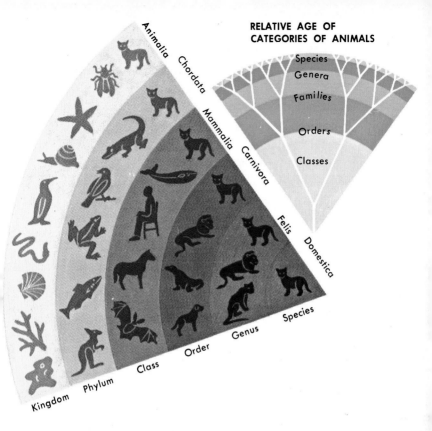

RELATIVE AGE OF CATEGORIES OF ANIMALS

Species
Genera
Families
Orders
Classes

Animalia
Chordata
Mammalia
Carnivora
Felis
Domestica

Kingdom
Phylum
Class
Order
Genus
Species

THE LINNAEAN TYPE CLASSIFICATION shows an increasing similarity of each group from the kingdom to the species. Note the modern evolutionary branching interpretation on the right.

IN BINOMIAL NOMENCLATURE, the basis of the classification developed by Linnaeus, each species has two names: the first is the genus to which it belongs; the second is the species. The Common Raven, for example, is Corvus corax, while the somewhat similar Common Crow is *Corvus brachyrhynchos.*

Linnaeus used this short, and internationally understood classification to classify all of the species known at that time.

LINNAEUS and most of his contemporaries assumed that each species was distinct and unchanging, their degrees of similarity reflecting similarity to the archetypes, or models, upon which each had been created.

11

THE VARYING DEGREES OF DIVERSITY shown by different species suggested to some eighteenth century students a conclusion boldly different from that reached by Linnaeus and most of his contemporaries. Perhaps, it was argued, species were not unchanging and immutable. Perhaps existing species arose by a slow modification of earlier forms. Perhaps degrees of similarity between species reflected their degree of relationship to common ancestral forms. Perhaps change, not constancy, was one essential characteristic of species. Perhaps species have evolved, or unfolded, rather than having appeared fully formed. Perhaps they arose not from a single creative act but by slow processes of change over long periods of time.

ERASMUS DARWIN (1731-1802), grandfather of Charles Darwin, was a physician, poet, and naturalist. He was impressed by the extent of changes in form within the lifetime of individual animals (frogs, for example), by the influence of selective breeding in horses and dogs, by differences due to climate, and by the close affinities of the mammals—which he reasoned implied their common origin.

JEAN BAPTISTE DE LAMARCK (1744-1829), French soldier and biologist, was the founder of the studies of invertebrate animals. He stressed that no absolute limits separated one species from another and that species retain constant characteristics only in unchanging environments. When the environment does change, he argued, the increased use of some organs and the relative disuse of

others lead to inheritable changes. The giraffe's long neck, for example, could be best explained by the long-continued habit of reaching upward to feed on the leaves of trees. By Lamarck's theory, the relative development of any organ responds to its degree of use.

Lamarck's belief that acquired characteristics can be inherited is no longer accepted, but his recognition of evolution was of major importance.

Lamarck's views suggested that giraffes reaching upward became increasingly longer-necked and transmitted this characteristic to their offspring.

The concepts of evolution proposed by Erasmus Darwin and by Lamarck were not only rejected but were also ridiculed by their scientific contemporaries. This was because of the excesses of some interpretations proposed by Lamarck and his disciples, and also because man's everyday experience provided little support for Lamarck's theory of species development. In spite of circumstantial evidence, no one had yet seen one species turn into another.

THE DISCOVERY THAT LIFE HAD A LONG HISTORY

did not come until the eighteenth and nineteenth centuries, when it became generally recognized that fossils were the remains of once-living animals and plants. Fossils indicated that many species had become extinct and that most living species were of recent origin. If species were immutable, how could these changes in the pattern of life be explained? During the nineteenth century, two opposing schools of thought developed.

CATASTROPHISTS attempted to reconcile the fossil record with the early chapters of the Book of Genesis. They regarded the Flood of Noah as the last of a series of great worldwide catastrophes, each of which destroyed all living things. After each catastrophe, a new creation took place, in which the earth was repopulated by animals and plants of new and different species. These in turn were destroyed, and their fossil remains entombed in the strata of the next cataclysm.

GRADUALISTS maintained that the fossil record showed no evidence of worldwide catastrophes, although it did show many examples of local erosion surfaces and changing environments of rock deposition. Although these changes are often marked by the cutoff of one kind of fossil and its replacement by another, this was a piecemeal, local, irregular process, not a worldwide one. New species originated, according to gradualists, by the slow modification of ancestral forms.

GEORGES CUVIER (1769-1832), an outstanding French anatomist and paleontologist, studied the fossil vertebrates of the Paris Basin. The succession of different species seemed to him to imply a series of universal catastrophes, the last of which was the Flood of Noah. Cuvier believed that some species survived to repopulate the earth while other students invoked a new creation after each of the catastrophes. As many as 30 catastrophes were proposed.

JAMES HUTTON (1726-1797), Scottish physician, landowner, and agriculturist, laid the foundations of modern geology. He recognized that many rocks were the result of erosion and deposition in environments that had modern counterparts. This concept of *uniformitarianism* sought to explain the features of the earth in terms of present processes.

CHARLES LYELL (1797-1875), a Scottish soldier, lawyer, and geologist, published *The Principles of Geology* in 1830-33 The book, which ran to twelve editions, had enormous influence. In it, Lyell established the science of geology, justifying and amplifying Hutton's concept of uniformitarianism. Lyell first used the word "evolution" in its present sense.

New discoveries led to the gradual rejection of catastrophism. First, the number of catastrophes required to explain the fossil record steadily increased until the whole system became unwieldly. It became clear, also, that the rock record could be interpreted satisfactorily in terms of present-day, observable geologic processes rather than unknown catastrophes. In addition, the "diluvial" rocks that lay over the surface of much of Europe and North America and were thought to be the remains of Noah's Flood were recognized as glacial deposits. More and more evidence of continuity (or evolution) of fossils was demonstrated. Darwin and Wallace proposed an acceptable mechanism for the process of evolution.

CHARLES DARWIN'S VOYAGE aboard the HMS *Beagle* changed the world's viewpoint in regard to evolution and the development of species. Until the publication of Darwin's *On the Origin of Species*, in 1859, the idea of evolution was generally rejected.

Darwin was born at Shrewsbury, England, on February 12, 1809, the same day as Lincoln. After two years of medical training at Edinburgh, he went to Cambridge, where he graduated in 1831. After his graduation, Darwin was appointed naturalist to the *Beagle*, a 240-ton, 10-gun brig, which was to undertake a survey voyage to South America and from there on around the world. The voyage lasted five years, and the insights Darwin gained during those years were to become the foundation of his life's work. Darwin made important contributions to the geology of South America, the origin of coral reefs, the relationships between living and fossil animals, and the structure, adaptation, and geographic distribution of animals. It was these studies that later formed the basis for his evolutionary theory.

DARWIN took the first volume of Lyell's newly published *Principles of Geology* on the voyage and was deeply impressed by it. Lyell argued that the earth's surface had been shaped by such natural forces as river erosion, volcanic eruptions, and changes in sea levels. Darwin used such ideas in unraveling the geology of areas he visited, and they influenced his thinking about the origin of species.

Charles Darwin, aged 31

Route of *The Beagle*

The route of the HMS *Beagle* is shown on the map above. It is probable that Darwin contracted Chagas' disease during an inland journey in South America, making him a semi-invalid later.

FOSSIL VERTEBRATES collected by Darwin from Argentina and elsewhere included *Toxodon*, a heavy elephant-sized mammal that looked much like a rhinoceros. Darwin concluded (wrongly) that it showed the two groups were closely related.

Darwin discovered fossil teeth of horses that had lived at the same time as *Toxodon* and had become extinct with it, although surviving in other parts of the world. This made the idea of catastrophic worldwide extinction appear suspect.

THE SIMILARITY of some fossil vertebrates, such as the giant armadillo-like *Glyptodon*, to forms still living suggested to Darwin the idea of descent by evolution.

Toxodon

Glyptodon

17

THE GALAPAGOS ISLANDS, located in the Pacific about 600 miles west of the coast of Ecuador, are a desolate group of 14 rocky islands, representing the remains of extinct volcanoes. The islands are separated from each other by deep water, and no winds or ocean currents carry small animals or seeds from one to another. The general absence of mammals has allowed giant tortoises to graze in safety, lizards to become seagoing, and finches to exist in niches that elsewhere are occupied by other species.

Darwin discovered that each of the islands, although having very similar climates and environments and being only about 50 miles apart, has its own fauna and flora — similar to but distinct from those of the neighboring islands. This suggested to Darwin that the similar species might have developed from a common ancestor rather than each having been created separately.

The islands are of recent origin, and their fauna, derived from the South American mainland, illustrates colonization of, and adaption to, an empty environment by relatively rapid evolution.

IGUANAS grow to four feet long and are fearsome in appearance, but they are harmless herbivores, feeding on seaweeds. Found only in the Galapagos Islands, they include two related species, one terrestrial, and the other marine. The latter are powerful swimmers, with webbed toes and a flattened tail to assist in swimming. Each island has its own race, showing minor differences from one group to another.

GIANT TORTOISES weighing up to 250 pounds graze on vegetation, filling a niche occupied in other places by mammals. These tortoises are found only in the Galapagos Islands, and each major island has its own variety. The variation *within* a single species of tortoise is so similar to that found between species in the Galapagos finches that Darwin wrote, "I must suspect that (the finch species) are only varieties."

THE FINCHES of the Galapagos Islands showed a general similarity to one another and to those of the mainland of South America, but the finches of each island differed slightly from those of the next. The 13 different species showed a perfect gradation, from ground-living, seed-eating forms with heavy, large beaks to tree-dwelling, insect-eating forms with long, pointed beaks.

Darwin wondered why the species, if created separately, resembled one another and those of the mainland of South America, whereas birds of the Cape Verde Islands, at the same latitude in the South Atlantic, resembled those of Africa. "One might really fancy," wrote Darwin, "that . . . one species had been taken and modified for different ends." These are illustrated on p. 82.

The Galapagos Islands, showing route of H.M.S. Beagle.

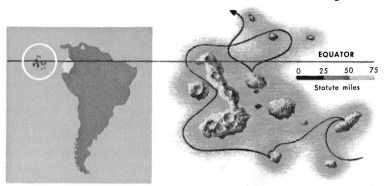

THE SEARCH FOR A MECHANISM had begun. Charles Darwin returned with the *Beagle* to England in October of 1836. The following July he opened his first notebook on *The Transmutation of Species*. He was then 27 years old. Darwin had seen how small variations could be selected by artificial breeding in domestic animals. Could the same transformations *within* a species also occur *between* species so that one ultimately gave rise to another? Darwin's observations suggested that they could, but he could not visualize the method.

ALFRED RUSSEL WALLACE (1832-1913), British surveyor and naturalist, independently suggested the theory of natural selection. Already convinced of the fact of evolution, he conceived the idea of natural selection while lying sick with fever in the Moluccas in February, 1858. He recalled the *Essay on Population*, by Robert Malthus, which he had read twelve years before. He wrote that he saw its application to evolution "in a flash of intuition."

Wallace was also an outstanding pioneer in the study of the geographic distribution of animals and its significance for the theory of evolution (p. 43).

ROBERT MALTHUS (1766-1834) was an English clergyman and economist. Unconvinced that man is perfect, and disbelieving the probability of universal peace, equality, and plenty, predicted by the politicians and utilitarian philosophers of the eighteenth century, Malthus wrote an anonymous "Essay on Population" in 1798. In it, he stated that human population cannot expand indefinitely. Populations expand at a geometric rate of increase with which food supplies can never keep pace. Famine, disease, and war, Malthus argued, will limit the increasing size of human populations.

Natural selection implies that ancestral giraffe populations included necks of various lengths. More of the longer-necked giraffes survived, and they produced increasing numbers of offspring that inherited their parents' longer necks.

"In October, 1838," wrote Darwin, "I happened to read Malthus for amusement. Being well prepared to appreciate the struggle for existence, which everywhere goes on, from long continued observation of the habits of animals and plants, it at once struck me that under these circumstances favorable variations would tend to be preserved and unfavorable ones to be destroyed. The result of this would be the formation of a new species."

Darwin called this process "natural selection." He argued that those particular individuals better adapted to their environment would live longer than the rest. Since the offspring would share their parents' characteristics, over many generations, those most favorable would tend to predominate. Darwin mulled over his theory, preparing a brief outline of it in 1842, and a longer abstract two years later. These were not published until 1858 (See p. 22). For the next fourteen years he gathered data for a four-volume treatise. These volumes were never published.

THE ORIGIN OF SPECIES. In the summer of 1858, Darwin received from Alfred Russel Wallace a manuscript entitled "On the Tendency of Varieties to Depart Indefinitely from the Original Type." Wallace had independently reached the conclusion that natural selection had played a major role in the origin of new species. Dismayed, Darwin offered to withdraw his own manuscript, but a joint paper by the two men was read before the Linnaean Society of London on July 1, 1858.

On November 24, 1859, Darwin published the *Origin of Species*—a brief abstract, as he called it, of his views. The book created a sensation. The first edition of 1250 copies sold out on the first day of publication. Scientists were at first divided in their views. Others, wrongly as it now appears, regarded the book as a direct challenge to religious beliefs. In such diverse fields as philosophy, history, anthropology, politics, and sociology, Darwin's book raised profound questions. The debate was widespread and intense.

THE ORIGIN OF SPECIES

BY MEANS OF NATURAL SELECTION,

OR THE

PRESERVATION OF FAVOURED RACES IN THE STRUGGLE FOR LIFE.

By CHARLES DARWIN, M.A.,

FELLOW OF THE ROYAL, GEOLOGICAL, LINNEAN, ETC., SOCIETIES;
AUTHOR OF 'JOURNAL OF RESEARCHES DURING H. M. S. BEAGLE'S VOYAGE
ROUND THE WORLD.'

LONDON:
JOHN MURRAY, ALBEMARLE STREET.
1859.

The right of Translation is reserved.

THE BOOK was carefully written and cogently argued. The first four chapters described the results of domestic selection and breeding and then developed the idea of natural selection. The fifth chapter, devoted to the mechanisms of variation and inheritance, is the only part of the book that has since been discredited. The sixth to tenth chapters discussed possible objections to the whole idea of evolution, and the remaining chapters treated possible evidence for evolution. Shown at left is the title page of the 1st edition.

Cartoonist's view, in 1871, of Charles Darwin (Left) and T. H. Huxley, (right) who championed his teachings.

The importance of Darwin's book on *The Origin of Species,* is difficult to exaggerate. It has been called the most important book of the nineteenth century. More than any other book, before or since, it established the theory of evolution—or "descent by modification," as Darwin called it. In this, Darwin initiated a transformation in the study of the organic world as profound as that brought about in the physical world by Newton's work with gravitation. In biology, evolution provided a powerful new unifying principle, giving new meaning and insight to a maze of conflicting data and also a new impetus in every field of inquiry.

The book's influence was not confined to biology. If life had a history, so had man, so had language, so had culture. Had they too evolved? If there had been organic evolution, had there also been inorganic evolution in which the earth, the solar system, the universe, matter, and energy itself had undergone change?

A watershed of human thought was established. Man's view of the world, of life, and of himself would never be quite the same again.

23

DARWIN'S THESIS for the origin of new species rested on three essential foundations—two of them demonstrable facts, the other an inference.

First, Darwin stressed that *variation* existed throughout the world of living things. No two individuals of the same species are exactly alike. In size, proportions, coloring, mental ability, disposition, physiological processes, and many other ways, each individual is unique. Furthermore, many of these and other features are transmitted from parent to offspring.

Secondly, Darwin argued that every species overproduces. More young are produced than ever survive, for the number of individuals in a population show relatively little variation. This overproduction exists at every level in the plant and animal kingdoms. "Even slow-breeding man," wrote Darwin, "has doubled (his numbers) in twenty-five years, and at this rate, in less than a thousand years there would literally not be standing room for his progeny." There must therefore be a very high rate of mortality, and this has been shown to be so. In many species of birds and insects, 98 percent of the individuals die before maturity.

Swarm of locusts exemplifies abundance of living things.

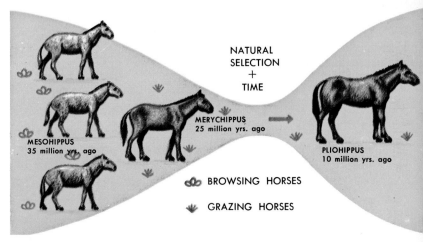

NATURAL
SELECTION
+
TIME

MERYCHIPPUS
25 million yrs. ago

MESOHIPPUS
35 million yrs. ago

PLIOHIPPUS
10 million yrs. ago

🦋 BROWSING HORSES

🌿 GRAZING HORSES

Darwin's "recipe" for evolution was the interaction of variation, overpopulation, and natural selection; illustrated here is evolution of horses (See p. 51).

Thirdly, Darwin argued that many characteristics of plants and animals were adaptations to the environments in which they lived. The protective coloring of many animals was clearly adaptive. The teeth of animals were clearly related to their diet, as were the beaks of birds. Whales, though mammals, were so adapted to life in the seas that they had fishlike bodies. Darwin suggested that these had come about by *natural selection* of favorable differences in ancestral organisms. Those best adapted to their environment would survive longer and so produce more offspring than those that were not. The offspring would inherit their parents' favorable characteristics. New species could develop in this way.

The vigorous debate that followed publication of Darwin's book saw gradual acceptance of his views. Darwin misunderstood the mechanism of variation and inheritance, but his general theory has withstood the test of time.

THE LAWS OF INHERITANCE, which had eluded Darwin and Wallace, were discovered by Gregor Mendel (1822-1884), an Austrian monk. Mendel is considered to be the founder of modern genetics. His work was published in 1866, but remained generally unknown until it was independently "rediscovered" by three biologists in 1900.

Mendel decided to study the inheritance of one or two readily recognizable characters in the garden pea—the size and form of the peas, their flower color, and so on. He cross-pollinated one form with another and then carefully recorded the results of this over several growing seasons. (p. 60)

MENDEL raised peas by cross-pollinating those with smooth, round peas and those with shriveled, wrinkled peas. He discovered that they did not produce a blending of the parent characters, as was generally believed, but that all the new peas were smooth and round. He then used these seeds to produce another crop, cross-pollinated them, and dis-covered that three-quarters of the new generation were smooth and round and one quarter was wrinkled.

Mendel called characters that could be masked in one generation but appear in another (such as wrinkled peas) *recessive;* those that overshadow them (such as the smooth, round pea form), *dominant.*

Mendel concluded that this delayed appearance of recessive characters must imply that each character is governed by an independent *factor* (which we now call a *gene)* and that these must be paired in the parent but not in the gametes.

Mendel made three major discoveries: (1) that characters are governed by paired but individual "factors," (2) that these factors may be dominant or recessive, and (3) that these factors combine, without blending, to produce characteristic ratios in the later generations.

Hugo de Vries, the discoverer of mutations, and the evening primrose that he used in his studies.

MUTATION. Mendel had shown that inheritance was particular and predictable. But if this was so, how could any new features ever arise? The answer was found partly in the action of natural selection and partly in the work of a Dutch botanist.

Hugo de Vries (1848-1935) was Professor of Botany at Amsterdam. He studied the mechanism of inheritance of characters in the evening primrose and became increasingly suspicious of the then current view that different parental characters always blended in the offspring and that all variations were small. He studied over 50,000 plants, and out of their several hundred thousand flowers, he discovered rare examples that were "sports." They had giant size or dwarf size, or twice the normal number of petals. When bred together, they produced similar offspring. Such new forms de Vries called *mutants,* the changes producing them *mutations.* In searching the literature, de Vries rediscovered the work of Mendel. These mutations provided the genuinely new characteristics upon which evolution by natural selection was dependent.

27

T. H. Morgan, a pioneer American geneticist.

Walter S. Sutton, geneticist who identified role of chromosomes.

THE NEW SYNTHESIS OF EVOLUTIONARY THEORY

came in the early years of the twentieth century, marked by recognition of *chromosomes,* minute thread-like structures in the cell nucleus, as the carriers of hereditary characters. This discovery, which also showed a linkage of characters that Mendel had not suspected, was made independently in 1902 by W. S. Sutton and by T. Boveri. T. H. Morgan (1886-1945), experimenting with the fruit fly, *Drosophila,* demonstrated that the genetic determinants were present in a definite linear order in the chromosomes and could be "mapped."

Many workers became convinced that it was sudden, spontaneous, large-scale mutations that were the real basis of evolution rather than, as Darwin had suggested, the minor variations. But why, others objected, should so many characters then be adaptive since many mutations proved to be lethal rather than beneficial? The discovery in 1927 that X-rays, temperature changes, gamma rays, and various chemicals could induce mutations proved that the great majority of them were minute in their effects and therefore were more likely to survive.

28

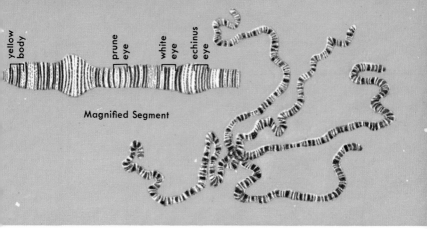

Chromosomes from the fruit fly *Drosophila* greatly magnified. The map shows location of genes along part of chromosome length.

The simple Mendelian concept of independent, particular genetic development has given way to acceptance of an individual represented by a gene complex in which genes are linked and interact together.

The current synthetic theory of evolution is based on rigorous statistical analysis, study of the fossil record, experimental studies, and observation of natural populations. It accepts as the basis for evolution individual variations, arising from mutation and reproductive recombination, and acted upon, filtered, conserved, intensified or eliminated by natural selection.

Genetic variation in *Drosophila* expressed by striking differences in form. The fly at left is the normal wild type.

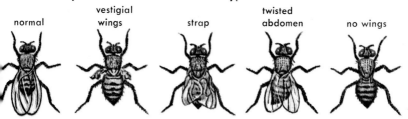

INDICATIONS OF EVOLUTION

The proof required for any particular statement varies with the nature of the statement. To prove that $2 + 2 = 4$ involves an appeal to reason and mathematical logic. To prove that an athlete can run a four-minute mile involves an appeal to experiment—the running of a carefully measured distance under specified conditions and with accurate timekeeping.

But no experiment could prove that the same athlete ran a four-minute mile on June 20th a year ago. Proof of that would involve an appeal to the record books and to witnesses. No experiment can provide proof of past events. Other kinds of evidence are needed, although observation and experiments of existing facts and processes may support the probability of a particular past event. Often proof involves an appeal to everyday experience to provide the most economical explanation. You could not prove, for example, that all of the sparrows living today descended from those living three hundred years ago, but the balance of experience would support that interpretation.

"I will believe in evolution," William Jennings Bryan remarked, "when I can sit in my garden and see an onion turn into a lily." Clearly, if we had to rely on that kind of instant experience, evolution could not be proved. But neither could the growth of an onion seed into an onion be proved instantly. It, too, is a slow scarcely perceptible event. We can, however, observe populations changing and can also observe the mechanisms by which such change comes about. The proof of evolution also lies in its unique position as the only adequate explanation for the origin of the diverse features shown by living things.

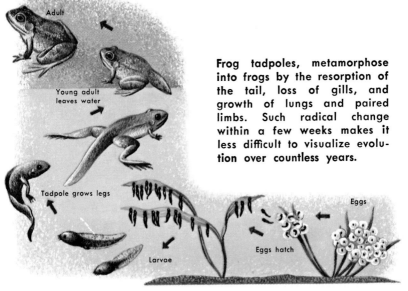

Frog tadpoles, metamorphose into frogs by the resorption of the tail, loss of gills, and growth of lungs and paired limbs. Such radical change within a few weeks makes it less difficult to visualize evolution over countless years.

Adult

Young adult leaves water

Tadpole grows legs

Larvae

Eggs hatch

Eggs

CONTINUITY of living things is provided by reproduction. Individuals live, grow old, and die, but their kind is perpetuated in their offspring. We know of no evidence suggesting that living organisms arise in any other way than from parents of the same species. It would be difficult to prove, for example, that all frogs alive today must have descended from frogs that lived 1,000 years ago, but all of our experience suggests that they have.

But if frogs always give birth to frogs and camels to camels, how do new kinds (species) of animals ever develop? Two features of continuity suggest possible answers. Firstly, continuity between parents and offspring involves both broad resemblances and individual differences and variations. Whatever explanation we select must explain both features.

Secondly, continuous change within the lifetime of a single individual animal is very great. If such changes can occur in one generation, it may well be that one species could develop into another.

UNITY OF LIFE is shown by the fact that, in spite of their diversity of form and variety of habits, the nearly 1 ½ million species of plants and animals all solve the basic problems of living in much the same way. They resemble one another in composition, cellular structure, life processes, and basic patterns of reproduction, adaptability, and development. They also share a common unity in the endless interdependence of all living things. If each species is an entirely separate creation, why do all share these basic common properties?

CELLULAR STRUCTURE is a characteristic of all living material, and the cells are made of protoplasm. Most cells are only a few thousandths of an inch in diameter, but a few are much larger. The yolks of bird eggs are single cells.

In spite of some differences, plant and animal cells do have a similar basic structure. Even the simplest cell consists of thousands of different molecules that interact together in coordination. A typical cell structure is shown below.

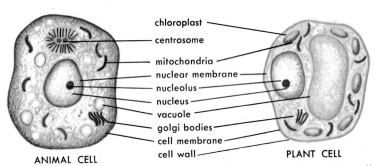

chloroplast
centrosome
mitochondria
nuclear membrane
nucleolus
nucleus
vacuole
golgi bodies
cell membrane
cell wall

ANIMAL CELL

PLANT CELL

PROTOPLASM

Oxygen	76.0%
Carbon	10.5%
Hydrogen	10.0%
Nitrogen	2.5%
Phosphorus	0.3%
Potassium	0.3%
Sulfur	0.2%
Chlorine	0.1%

PROTOPLASM is shared by all living things. It is composed of a distinctive combination of large molecules of nonliving substances, including carbohydrates, fats, proteins (including enzymes), and nucleic acids that are organized into a colloidal mixture in water. The unique properties of this material form the basis of life.

METABOLISM includes the nutrition, respiration, synthesis, and excretion that is characteristic of all living things. Non-living food materials are converted into the organism's living tissues, certain of which break down to provide the energy that is vital to the processes essential to life. Metabolism involves a constant flow of energy and materials within and between an organism and its environment.

REPRODUCTION of new duplicate individuals is characteristic of all living things. The continuity of form involved in reproduction is controlled by the activity of self-duplicating chemical structures called genes (p. 56).

GROWTH of newborn individuals is a common property of all living things.

ADAPTATION of all living things involves continuing adjustment to a changing environment. Individual adaptive responses include reaction to stimuli, irritability, physiologic changes, healing of injuries, and movement. Over long periods, populations show more general adaptations.

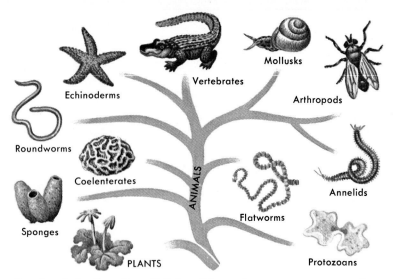

Despite their diversity, all living things share common properties.

THE NATURE OF LIFE is understood largely in terms of a series of fundamental properties (pp. 32-33).

No simple definition of "life" is possible, partly because of its complexity and partly because it is unique. But we can define life in terms of some of its simpler properties. Living organisms consist of unique and complex combinations of certain nonliving materials, arranged in large molecules that are capable of growth, reproduction, adaptation, and the gathering and using of external food and energy.

Some of these individual properties of living things are also present in nonliving things, but only living organisms exhibit them all simultaneously.

Other kinds of definitions of life are possible and are equally valid. Scientific definitions or studies are largely concerned with *how* life developed and *how* it is maintained. Philosophical and religious definitions are more concerned with *why*. The two kinds of definitions are usually complementary, not competitive.

INTERDEPENDENCE is a characteristic of all living things. Every individual exists as part of an interbreeding population that consists of many genetically similar individuals. These populations of individuals exist within communities of many species that interact with one another as prey and predator, host and parasite, consumer and producer, and competitors for space or food. The interaction cuts across the major divisions of plants and animals; thus, trees shelter birds, insects fertilize flowers, herbivores consume grass, fish support parasites, sea anemones shelter clown fish, etc.

COMMUNITIES interact with their physical environment, constituting an ecosystem. Changes in rainfall, temperature range, soil type, elevation, latitude, depth of sea water, sediment in streams, and countless other physical factors all influence the development of communities. Organisms in turn may modify their environment, creating local shade in forests, modifying and enriching soils, preventing erosion, and in many other ways. This interdependence provides important data.

Oxygen and carbon cycles show interdependence of all life.

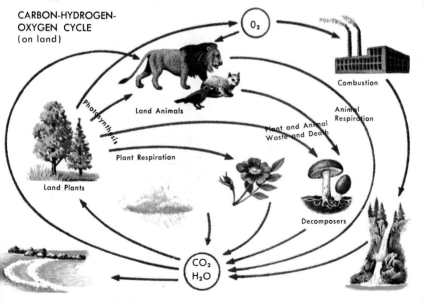

CARBON-HYDROGEN-OXYGEN CYCLE (on land)

O_2

Combustion

Photosynthesis

Land Animals

Animal Respiration

Plant and Animal Waste and Death

Plant Respiration

Land Plants

Decomposers

CO_2
H_2O

THE SIMILARITIES that exist between living organisms at all levels have certain implications. Offspring of the same parents have a more or less close resemblance to one another and to their parents. Although each individual is unique, members of the same species share "obvious" common features that are conserved and perpetuated in reproduction. We do not have trouble recognizing a lion, for example—or even a dog, despite the many variations that domestic breeding has produced in dogs.

DEGREES of resemblance also exist among related species. Ocelots, pumas, bobcats, and domestic cats, for example, all have certain basic characteristics in common, and these are recognized in animal classification (taxonomy) by grouping them all together in the same genus—*Felis*. But genera, too, exhibit degrees of resemblance so that we can group them into families of similar members. Similar families are grouped into orders, orders into classes, and classes into phyla. Each "higher" group thus includes more forms, and these have progressively fewer features in common (p. 11).

The orioles below belong to a single genus, *Icterus*. They have different colors and geographic ranges, but they share many common features. They are members of the same family as blackbirds.

I. spurius

I. graduacauda

I. parisorum

I. bullockii

I. galbula

I. cucullatus

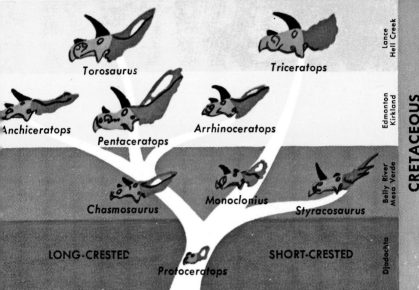

Torosaurus

Triceratops

Anchiceratops

Pentaceratops

Arrhinoceratops

Chasmosaurus

Monoclonius

Styracosaurus

LONG-CRESTED

SHORT-CRESTED

Protoceratops

Lance
Hell Creek

Edmonton
Kirkland

Belly River
Mesa Verde

Djadochta

These horned ceratopsian dinosaurs show how degrees of resemblance suggest evolutionary relationships. The geologic progression is arranged from bottom to top. (After Colbert.)

The meaning of the various degrees of resemblance was at first thought to lie in their approximation to the archetype or ideal form, upon which each species had been "designed" or planned. But to later students, these clustered relationships, often pictured as the branches of a tree (as above) suggested only degrees of relationship, although the classification itself was established before this was recognized (pp. 10-11). Just as the branches of a tree grow by continuous development from a seed, each branch being formed by slow and almost imperceptible modification of earlier branches from an initial stem, so the branching pattern of classification suggested a common origin. The branches represented degrees of relationship to the organisms of the central ancestral stem.

37

DEGREES OF SIMILARITY between living things are reflected by various features. The overall form and structure (morphology) of all creatures show varying degrees of similarity. When we speak of a "deer," we think of a particular kind of animal, but the deer family contains 20 different genera and many species. Although they differ in size, antlers, color, and geographic distribution, all members of the deer family share basic features. Their skeletons resemble one another, bone for bone; their internal organs are similar; and they display many similar behavioral characteristics. This comprehensive similarity, showing a unity of basic form but a diversity of individual pattern, suggests their derivation from a common ancestor that possessed these common features.

THE EMBRYONIC DEVELOPMENT of many species shows startling similarities, even in forms that have few resemblances as adults. Thus a man, a pig, and a chicken have a general similarity during their development. If each species is entirely distinct from every other species, it makes no sense that they should have such embryonic resemblances and then lose them in adult life. Although this embryonic similarity is less than was claimed by late nineteenth century zoologists, it is an indication and an imprint of their remote kinship.

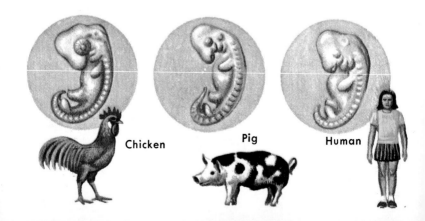

Chicken   Pig   Human

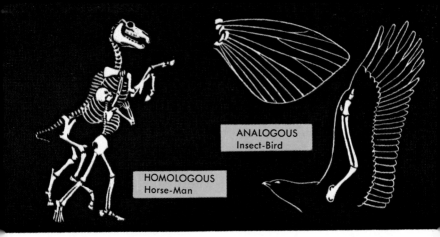

ANALOGOUS
Insect-Bird

HOMOLOGOUS
Horse-Man

HOMOLOGOUS STRUCTURES in many organisms suggest their derivation from common ancestors. The skeletons of cats, horses, whales, bats, mice, and men, for example, all have an essentially similar form. The structure of the vertebrae and the fused bones of the skull are similar in every vertebrate, from fish to men. So are the related nerves, muscles, and blood vessels. In less closely related species, homology is less well marked, suggesting their more distant community of origin.

ANALOGOUS STRUCTURES show a similarity of function but not of detailed structure. The wings of an insect perform the same function as those of a bird, but they have a very different structure. Such differences result not from inheritance from a common ancestor but from adaptation to similar environmental conditions. If each species had a separate origin, then analogous structures should be more common than homologous structures, but the reverse is true.

VESTIGIAL STRUCTURES develop when an organ is retained even though its original function is reduced or lost. Such structures are found in all animals. In man, the ear muscles are usually nonfunctional, but in other animals, such as the dog, these muscles move the ears and direct them toward particular sounds. The human appendix has no obvious function and is a nuisance, but in other animals, the appendix is more strongly developed and serves an

important digestive function. In whales and in some snakes, vestigial hind limbs are preserved, suggesting that they are the remnants of ancestral structures.

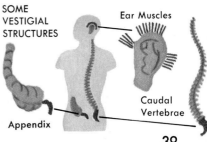

SOME VESTIGIAL STRUCTURES

Ear Muscles

Appendix

Caudal Vertebrae

39

BIOCHEMICAL SIMILARITIES also exist between related organisms. The most striking feature of these similarities is the way they confirm independently the various groupings of plants and animals that were established on the basis of their overall form. This implies that the classification that has been developed (pp. 36-37) is not wholly artificial but reflects the ancestral-descendant (phylogenetic) relationships of organisms.

Other more general biochemical similarities imply the common kinship of all organisms. These include the use of nucleic acids as agents of heredity (p. 68), the use of a particular phosphate, ATP, in energy transfer, and the use by plants with chlorophyll of this green pigment as a catalyst in photosynthesis.

BLOOD PIGMENTS differ in different animal groups. In vertebrates and some other animals, the blood has a red pigment, hemoglobin, which has a respiratory function in carrying blood from the lungs or gills throughout the body. In all arthropods, the respiratory pigment is a blue copper compound, called hemocyanin; in marine worms, a green iron compound, called chlorocruorine. These pigment similarities confirm the relationships between members of the groups established by other criteria. Proteins of each species, although distinct, show comparable degrees of similarity.

A serological test (p. 41) is made by mixing serum and antiserum and recording the highest dilution of serum that will still give a white ring of precipitate. (After Boyden.)

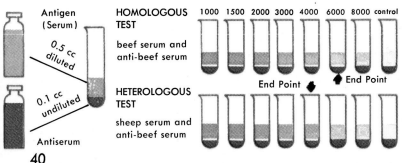

40

SEROLOGICAL SIMILARITIES are measured by immunity tests. If blood from one species, such as a cow, is injected into the bloodstream of another, say a guinea pig, the guinea pig produces a precipitate, an antiserum, that immunizes it against cow's blood. When this anti-cow serum is mixed with the blood of other animals, it produces precipitates of varying intensity that correspond to the nearness of the other species in the scheme of classification. Thus, anti-cow serum gives 100 percent precipitation with the blood of another cow, 48 percent with a sheep, and 24 percent with a pig. This biochemical indication of common ancestry is a method of classification confirming what was established independently by comparative anatomical studies.

Serological tests made with anti-human serum give varying percentages of precipitation. This reflects the quantitative degrees of similarity between man and other species.

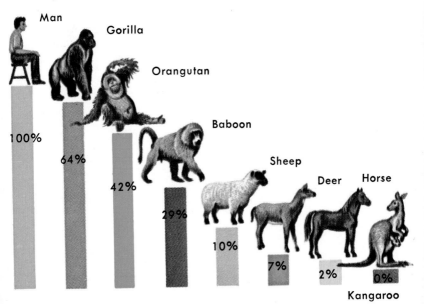

Man 100%
Gorilla 64%
Orangutan 42%
Baboon 29%
Sheep 10%
Deer 7%
Horse 2%
Kangaroo 0%

ADAPTATIONS to the particular environments in which they live are shown by all living creatures. Some that are so general they may be overlooked easily include the wonderfully efficient but distinct wing structure of insects, bats, and birds (also those of the extinct pterodactyls), the shape and structure of fish, the specialized stems of desert cacti, and countless others. Still other adaptations are more specific. Of the many examples among birds, those of the woodpeckers were first described by Charles Darwin.

Adaptation is so widespread in both plants and animals that, although not a proof of evolution, it suggests that natural selection is a very probable explanation for organic diversity.

PROTECTIVE form and coloration are adaptations shown by many animals. The pupae of some insects resemble thorns or twigs. Others mimic less vulnerable species by color resem- blances. The color of some animals, such as the chameleon, changes with the color of the background. Experiments have shown the survival value of this coloration (p. 84):

Chameleon

Woodpecker

A woodpecker has two large toes directed backward so that its foot forms an anchorlike hold. Its stiff tail feathers form a prop as the bird chisels with its powerful beak. It extracts insects with its long, barbed tongue. All of the 179 species of woodpeckers have essentially similar structure.

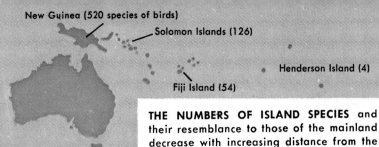

New Guinea (520 species of birds)

Solomon Islands (126)

Henderson Island (4)

Fiji Island (54)

THE NUMBERS OF ISLAND SPECIES and their resemblance to those of the mainland decrease with increasing distance from the land. The number of mammal species shows a similar decrease, suggesting that the species were derived from those on the mainland.

PRESENT LIMITED DISTRIBUTION OF MANY SPECIES, such as tapirs, can be interpreted only on the assumption that they are descendants of more widespread fossil ancestors, some of which have been found in intermediate areas.

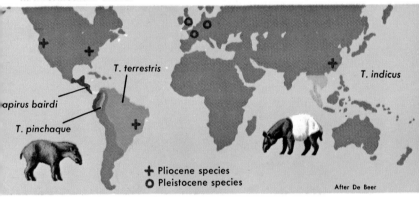

T. terrestris

T. indicus

apirus bairdi

T. pinchaque

✚ Pliocene species
◯ Pleistocene species

After De Beer

GEOGRAPHIC DISTRIBUTION of many plants and animals shows features that can be accounted for only by supposing that they are the descendants of common ancestors. The faunas of the Galapagos and Cape Verde Islands were major clues in Darwin's development of an evolutionary theory (pp. 18-19).

Alfred Russel Wallace noted that larger groups, such as orders, have a wider geographic distribution than do smaller groups, such as families or genera. Species most similar are found in adjacent areas, suggesting their evolution from common ancestors.

LIVING SPECIES of plants and animals are characterized by their constancy of general form and their great range of individual variation. Each species breeds "true" and is reproductively isolated from other species, even those that are closely similar. Yet no two individuals of the same species are identical. We now recognize that the inherited characteristics of all living things are controlled by their genes and chromosomes and that these structures undergo spontaneous mutations (p. 74). This input of new characteristics means that over a long period of time species are not fixed entities as once supposed. Both in nature and in captivity, we see evidence of variations within a species, suggesting their evolutionary capacity.

SELECTIVE BREEDING of domestic plants and animals indicates the great variability of many species. Illustrated here, are dogs of the same species.

This suggested to Darwin that natural selection might be analogous in its action to (artificial) domestic selection as an agent of change.

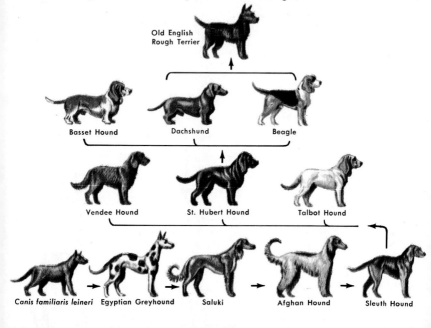

Old English
Rough Terrier

Basset Hound   Dachshund   Beagle

Vendee Hound   St. Hubert Hound   Talbot Hound

Canis familiaris leineri   Egyptian Greyhound   Saluki   Afghan Hound   Sleuth Hound

POPULATIONS show local variation in nature. The smallest units, called *demes*, are only partly isolated populations, within which there is close genetic similarity. Variation between demes is often random, but between some it is non-random, forming graded clines that may show correlation with different ecologic conditions. Thus local *races* or *subspecies* develop, each adapted to the conditions of a particular area and intergrading with one another only in overlapping areas.

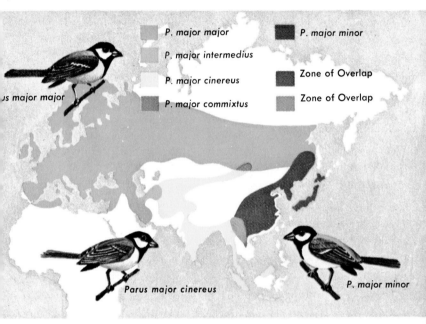

Geographical Distribution of the Great Tit. (After De Beer)

The Great Tit of Europe and Asia shows development of typical geographic races or varieties. The most widespread race is *Parus major major*, extending from Britain to East Asia. *P. cinereus* and *P. minor* have more restricted ranges.

The interbreeding in Iran of *P. major* with the central Asian and Indian variety *P. cinereus* gives a fourth variety—*P. intermedius*. Interbreeding of *P. cinereus* and *P. minor* in Indochina gives a fifth, *P. commixtus*. But *P. major* and *P. cinereus* occur together without interbreeding in north central Asia, as do *P. minor* and *P. major* in northeastern China. Reproductive isolation between geographic races suggests one mechanism for the formation of new species (p. 76).

45

CHANGES IN SPECIES have been observed even during the limited time that accurate observations have been recorded. Some disease-producing bacteria have been successfully treated with drugs, but one of the side effects of this medication has been the development of various drug resistant strains of the bacteria. *Escherichia coli* is a common bacterium that has developed populations entirely resistant to streptomycin. These resistant groups arise from mutations. When they appear, they are the only group able to survive and multiply.

Although most evolution is probably the result of slow, cumulative change, by this process of "preadaptation" in which a mutation "encounters" a favorable environment, the whole character of a population may change very rapidly. By a similar process, some species of destructive insects have developed an immunity to various insecticides. Scale insects of the citrus regions of California have become increasingly resistant to hydrocyanic acid, for example.

A scale insect, *Aonidella aurantii*.

INDUSTRIAL MELANISM has been observed in scores of species of moths during the past century. In industrial areas, many species have become progressively darker, or even black, while members of the same species in rural areas remain light colored. This demonstrates how plastic and changeable many species are, even over short periods of time. The mechanism of this change is discussed on p. 84. In the photograph below, the lichen-covered tree trunk provides concealment for the light-colored Peppered Moth but makes the darker, industrial melanic form conspicuous. The soot-covered tree trunk from an industrial area conceals the dark form of the Peppered Moth but makes the light form conspicuous.

credit: H. B. D. Kettlewell

Peppered moth, *Biston betularia*, showing light and dark forms on two different backgrounds.

FOSSIL SPECIES are difficult to recognize because the test of reproductive isolation, by which living species are distinguished, cannot be used. But we can recognize in fossils the same degrees of structural difference as between related living species. We can also recognize independently developing fossil groups, and these, by definition, can be regarded as species.

The fossil record allows us to observe changes over far longer periods of time than are ever available in living populations. In fossils, we can recognize evolution in action. Although they tell us little about the detailed mechanisms of change, fossils do provide powerful evidence that evolution has occurred.

FORAMINIFERA are microscopic protozoans, most of which secrete a shell. Illustrated is a marine genus, *Textularia*, studied in rocks of Tertiary age (p. 98) in New Zealand. When traced through a period represented by the accumulation of 500 feet of strata, there is a marked change in shape for each population. Two species are recognized. Horizontal lines represent standard deviation for each. (After Kennett.)

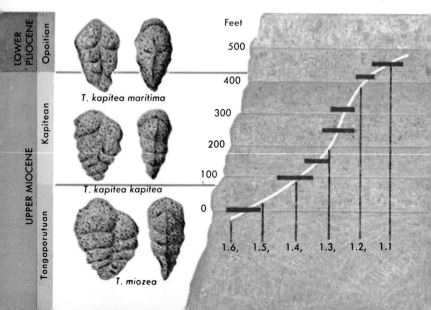

Fossil bivalve clams (below), from rocks of Pennsylvanian and Permian age (p. 98) of the midcontinent region of the United States, show successive development by descent of closely similar species of the genus *Myalina*. Each of the numbers on graphs represents a different species, listed below.

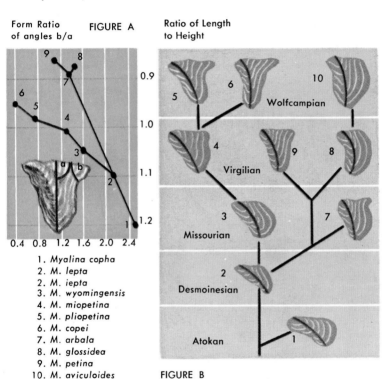

Form Ratio of angles b/a   FIGURE A   Ratio of Length to Height

1. *Myalina copha*
2. *M. lepta*
2. *M. iepta*
3. *M. wyomingensis*
4. *M. miopetina*
5. *M. pliopetina*
6. *M. copei*
7. *M. arbala*
8. *M. glossidea*
9. *M. petina*
10. *M. aviculoides*

FIGURE B

Figure A is a plot of the form ratio of length to height of the shells, plotted against the ratio of the angle b to the angle a (see diagram). The right-hand line represents in-line evolution, where new species arise by successive modification of earlier populations. The left-hand line represents speciation by branching or splitting rather than by continuous change.

Figure B shows inferred evolutionary descent and relationships (phylogeny) of species of *Myalina*. Numbers refer to the same species as those in Fig. A. The names are those of successive rock divisions. (After Newell and Moore.)

49

HIGHER TAXA (genera, families, etc.) of animals and plants are found in the fossil record also to arise by descent with slow modification from ancestral forms. This is evolution. The fossil record provides repeated evidence that it is the normal method by which new groups of organisms originate.

CERATOPSIAN DINOSAURS (all drawn to same scale) lived in the Cretaceous Period (p. 98), 70 million years ago. They show an overall increase in size and in the relative dimensions and complexity of the bony armor that covered their head and neck, *Triceratops* reached a length of 24 feet and weighed up to eight tons. Only three genera are shown. (After Colbert.)

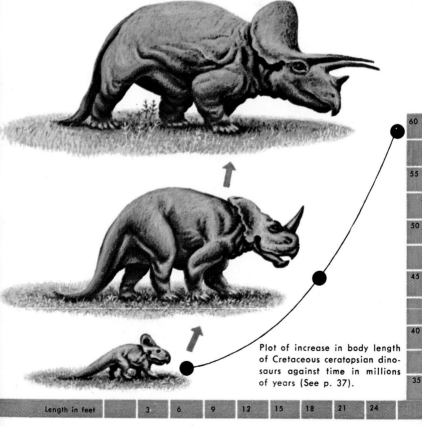

Plot of increase in body length of Cretaceous ceratopsian dinosaurs against time in millions of years (See p. 37).

60

55

50

45

40

35

Length in feet   3   6   9   12   15   18   21   24

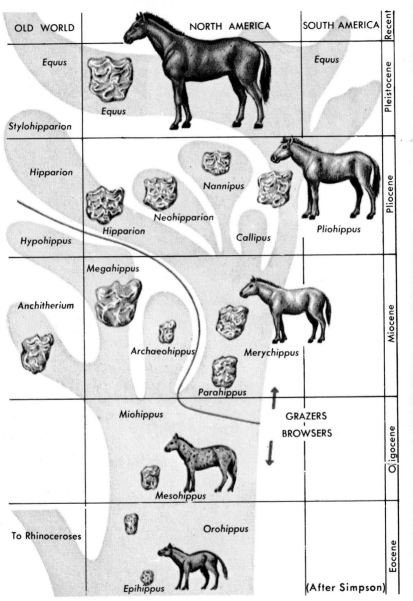

OLD WORLD	NORTH AMERICA	SOUTH AMERICA	
			Recent
Equus		Equus	Pleistocene
	Equus		
Stylohipparion			
Hipparion	Nannipus		Pliocene
	Neohipparion		
Hypohippus	Hipparion	Pliohippus	
	Callipus		
	Megahippus		Miocene
Anchitherium	Archaeohippus	Merychippus	
	Parahippus		
	Miohippus	GRAZERS BROWSERS	Oligocene
	Mesohippus		
To Rhinoceroses	Orohippus		Eocene
	Epihippus	(After Simpson)	

HORSES provide a classic example of the evolution of new genera from earlier ones over a period of 70 million years. Later modifications reflected change in diet from browsing to grazing. Right upper molar tooth surfaces are shown.

51

"MISSING LINKS," as evidence that one group developed from another, were often demanded by opponents of evolution in earlier years of the evolutionary debate. At the time of the publication of *On the Origin of Species,* very few of these transitional forms were known, but many have since been discovered. They bridge many of the major groups of existing organisms. In the vertebrates, for example, there are transitional forms between fish and amphibia, amphibia and reptiles, reptiles and birds, and reptiles and mammals. They indicate that these major groups, distinct and separate in living forms, arose from forms that showed some characters intermediate between two groups and others now restricted to just one.

ARCHAEOPTERYX, an ancestral fossil bird from the Jurassic of Germany, had many features of the reptilian group from which it developed. Although it had the feathers of a bird, it had a reptilelike toothed beak and clawed wings. It had birdlike feet but reptilian vertebrae and tail. It had the wishbone of a bird but a reptilian brain. *Archaeopteryx* was indeed a mosaic or jumble of variously developed characteristics that were subsequently restricted to different groups (p. 129).

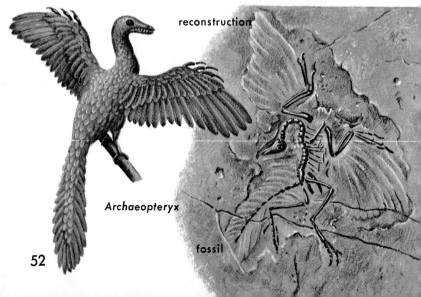

reconstruction

Archaeopteryx

fossil

Cynognathus

THE THERIODONTS "beast-toothed") were reptiles that lived in Permian and Triassic times (p. 98). They showed many mammalian characteristics. *Cynognathus* was a typical member of the group. An active carnivore, six feet long, it had a long skull with mammal-like differentiation of the teeth into incisors, canines, and cheek teeth. It had an "upright" mammalian posture, and many details of the skull, vertebrae, hips, shoulders, and limbs were also mammal-like. Mammals are believed to have developed from these or similar reptiles.

Platypus

LIVING FOSSILS are surviving representatives of ancient fossil groups. The monotremes—the duckbilled platypus and the spiny anteaters (echidnas) of Australia—are very primitive mammals that retain many typical reptilian characters in their skeletons. They lay leathery, large-yolked eggs and secrete milk from modified sweat glands. Such animals probably arose from transitional reptilian-mammalian forms. Ginkgos and araucarias are plant living fossils.

53

THE FOSSIL RECORD shows three other general features which suggest that species arose by continuous evolution. It displays diversification, environment-filling, and complex adaptational change. These are precisely what would be predicted, *a priori*, on the basis of the theory of evolution.

THE ADAPTATION OF ORGANISMS to a greater range of environments has developed with time. The oldest organisms were confined to the seas, but fresh waters, the land, and the air were successively colonized. Details are given on p. 118 and the following pages.

The history of the vertebrates shows an increasing range of adaptation. Birds and a few mammals and extinct reptiles have colonized the air; others have "returned" to the aquatic life abandoned by their ancestors. Detailed adaptations have developed in each environment.

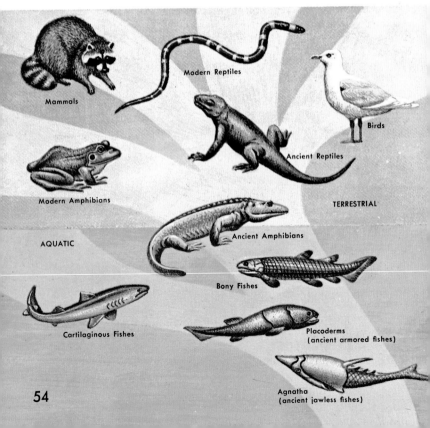

Mammals

Modern Reptiles

Birds

Modern Amphibians

Ancient Reptiles

TERRESTRIAL

AQUATIC

Ancient Amphibians

Bony Fishes

Cartilaginous Fishes

Placoderms
(ancient armored fishes)

Agnatha
(ancient jawless fishes)

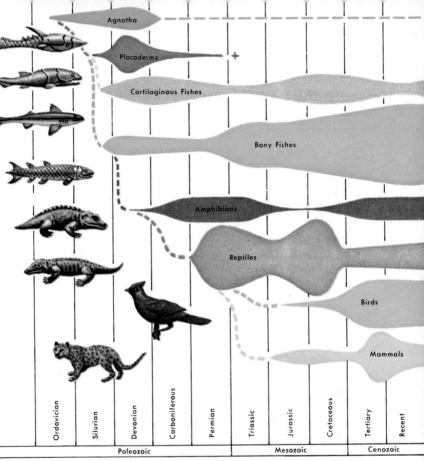

The classes of vertebrates show an increase in complexity and diversity with time. The width of the columns indicates the relative abundance of each group; dotted lines show the probable origin of each group. (After Simpson)

THE TOTAL NUMBER of species has shown a steady increase through geologic time. Insects, for example, constitute more than three-quarters of all living species, yet they did not appear until the Devonian, 375 million years ago (p. 98). The classes (above) shows increasing numbers of species.

GREATER COMPLEXITY of organisms with time has accompanied the invasion of new environments. "Complexity" is an ambiguous quality, but most would agree that fish, amphibians, reptiles, and mammals represent such a scale. This is also the order of their appearance in the fossil record.

THE PROCESS OF EVOLUTION

INHERITANCE provides the constancy of form (a lion is a lion is a lion) and variation in detail (blue eyes, green eyes, brown eyes, black eyes) that are characteristic of all living plants and animals. Lobsters produce only lobsters; humans produce humans. But no two lobsters and no two humans are ever identical in all characteristics. How are these two, constancy and variety, transmitted from parents to offspring?

GENES, as demonstrated by Gregor Mendel (p. 26) and by subsequent students of genetics, are the regulators that govern the development of characteristics in new individuals. Genes are made of deoxyribonucleic acid—DNA (pp. 72-75)—and *reproduce* themselves exactly.

Genes are incorporated in visible structures called chromosomes, each of which contains many genes. Each species has a definite type and number of chromosomes. In all but the most simple organisms, the chromosomes are contained in the cell nucleus. Characteristics of an organism are governed by particular genes; but individual genes may interact with one another or combine to produce continuous variation of some characters.

The human chromosomes shown below carry genes that determine individual characteristics. X and Y are the sex chromosomes.

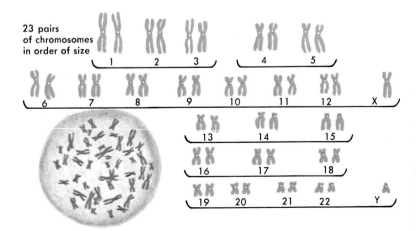

23 pairs of chromosomes in order of size

1 2 3   4 5

6 7 8 9 10 11 12 X

13 14 15

16 17 18

19 20 21 22 Y

chromosomes in spermatogonium

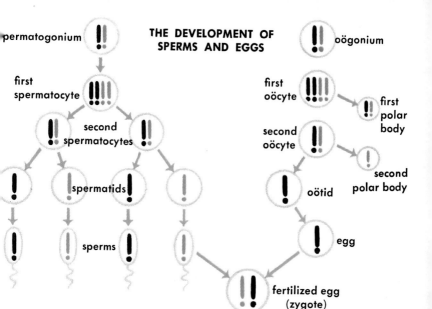

THE DEVELOPMENT OF SPERMS AND EGGS

GAMETES are the specialized reproductive cells of plants and animals. Most species produce both male gametes (sperm) and female gametes (eggs).

Each gamete contains only one chromosome from each pair of the organism's diploid cells. Unlike the body cells, which have a diploid or 2n chromosome number, the total number of chromosomes in a gamete is n. These cells with unpaired chromosomes are called haploid.

CHROMOSOMES of most species occur in pairs so that each cell contains two similar (homologous) chromosomes. Each chromosome in turn contains homologous genes. Such cells are called diploid. The diploid number indicates the total number of chromosomes that these cells contain.

In man, for example, most cells contain 23 chromosomes, hence the usual chromosome number (n) is 23. But since the chromosomes are paired in diploid cells, the total diploid number in each cell is 2n or 46.

CELL DIVISION—the constant manufacture of new cells—is essential for the life and growth of all multicellular plants and animals. Injured or worn out cells are replaced by this process, too. The new cells are exact replicas of the original cells, containing the same kind and number of chromosomes.

The process of producing new cells by division of the original cell is called mitosis. In most cell division, the process is completed in less than two hours. Mitosis can produce new individuals as well as new body cells. In most organisms that reproduce asexually, the new cell is identical to the parent cell.

MITOSIS

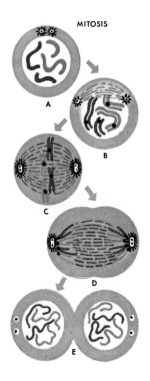

A

B

C

D

E

THE STAGES OF MITOSIS include: (a) PROPHASE, first stage of mitosis, is marked by thickening of chromosomes in nucleus and separation of centrioles from central body (centrosome) above nucleus. Fibers from centrioles form aster. (b) SPINDLE of fibers then grows between the two separated asters. Nuclear membrane disintegrates, and the thickened chromosomes divide lengthwise into two chromatids. (c) IN METAPHASE, the duplicated chromosomes leave the nucleus. They arrange themselves into pairs across the equator of the enlarged spindle. (d) IN ANAPHASE, one of each of the chromosomes pairs, or chromatid, migrates to opposite poles of the spindle. (e) TELOPHASE, final stage, is marked by loss of spindle, division of centriole, and division of parent cell into two identical daughter cells.

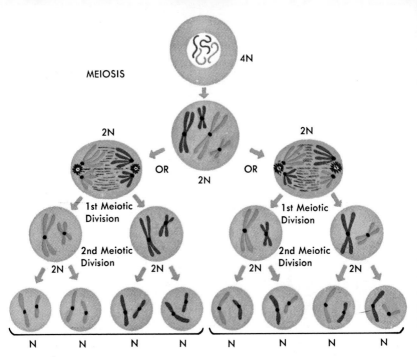

MEIOSIS

4N

2N 2N

OR OR

2N

1st Meiotic Division · 1st Meiotic Division

2nd Meiotic Division · 2nd Meiotic Division

2N · 2N · 2N · 2N

N   N   N   N   N   N   N   N

MEIOSIS is shown for a cell with a diploid number (2N) of four chromosomes. The first division involves the random sharing of exactly half the number of chromosomes between the daughter cells. In this reduction division, the sharing of the original chromosomes may produce either of two combinations in the haploid daughter cells, each of which has N chromosomes—that is, half of the original number of chromosomes.

The second division occurs by mitosis, in which each new daughter cell divides into two further haploid cells, each also with N chromosomes. These form the gametes, or reproductive cells, each of which has one chromosome from each of the original pairs. The union of two gametes, each of which has the haploid or N chromosome number, gives the offspring the original 2N chromosome number of the parents.

SEXUAL REPRODUCTION involves a second and different kind of cell division, called meiosis. In sexually reproducing organisms, meiosis is confined to the testis of the male and to the ovary of the female. All the other cells of the body increase in number by mitosis. Meiosis involves two distinct stages of cell division.

59

THE PATTERNS OF INHERITANCE were first demonstrated by Gregor Mendel (p. 26) with seven easily recognized characters in garden peas (size, shape, color of flowers, and so on). In studying their occurrence through successive generations, he discovered that characters are controlled by factors (now called genes) that do not blend in the offspring. He also discovered that in the second generation some characters, such as short stems, yellow color, and wrinkled peas, may be masked by others, such as long stems, green color, and round shape. The masked features will reappear in the third generation. He called these characters *dominant* and *recessive* and concluded that they are inherited independently of one another.

THE INHERITED RATIO of one character to another was shown by Mendel to be constant. He cross-pollinated purebred round pea plants (R) with purebred wrinkled pea plants (r). The F_1 (first filial) generation peas were all round, but those in the next generation (F_2) included 25 percent wrinkled, as shown here.

RR   Parents   rr

R   Gametes   r

F_1 Offspring

Rr   Mating F_1 Rr

R   r   R   r

RR   Rr   Rr   rr

1. Pure Dominant   2. Mixed   1. Pure Recessive

Mendel concluded that each plant had a pair of genes for each character, because some plants (such as those of the F_1) with a dominant character produced some offspring with the recessive character. F_1 plants are shown as Rr on the diagram. Purebred plants, also with paired genes, are RR or rr.

Mendel reasoned that these paired genes must separate to form gametes. At fertilization, they unite randomly with other gametes, producing a predictable ratio of characteristics in the offspring. Many features may be influenced by more than two kinds of contrasting characters, called alleles, in each gene. Continuously varying characteristics, like height, are accounted for partly by this and partly by the fact that several different pairs of genes may control the same character.

The genotype of any organism is its total complement of genetic materials. The physical characteristics of an organism are called its *phenotype*. The genotype Rr produces the phenotype of round peas.

THREE GENOTYPES—RR, Rr, and rr—are shown in plants of the F_1 generation on p. 60. A plant with a pair of the same genes for a particular character (RR and rr) is called *homozygous*, meaning "same pair." One with a pair of different genes in the genotype (Rr) is *heterozygous*, or "different pair." Genes of the same gene pair—R and r, for example, are alleles.

Because of the dominance of some characters, organisms with the same phenotype may have different genotypes. Round peas, for example, may have genotypes of either RR or R. Only by studying their offspring can we distinguish between them. Homozygous (RR) plants will breed true, producing all R offspring. Heterozygous plants' produce both R and r offspring.

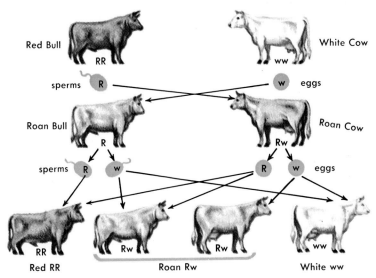

Red Bull
RR

White Cow
ww

sperms R

w eggs

Roan Bull
R

Roan Cow
Rw

sperms R w

R w eggs

RR
Red RR

Rw Rw
Roan Rw

ww
White ww

BLENDING OF SOME CHARACTERS may occur when one allele is not completely dominant over the other. In shorthorn cattle, a red bull (RR) and a white cow (ww) produce heterozygous calves that are roan (a mixture of red and white hairs). Crossing a roan bull (Rw) and a roan cow (Rw) gives a probable ratio of 1 white, 2 roan, and 1 red.

61

THE LAWS OF INHERITANCE are demonstrated below by the interaction of two different characters in studies of a combination of pea plant size (T = tall, dominant; and t = dwarf, recessive) and pea shape (R = round, dominant; r = wrinkled, recessive). Crossing a pure round-seeded, tall plant (RT) with a pure wrinkle-seeded, dwarf plant (rt) gives the results shown. Mendel's simple ratios were obtained by averaging the results of crossing large numbers of different plants.

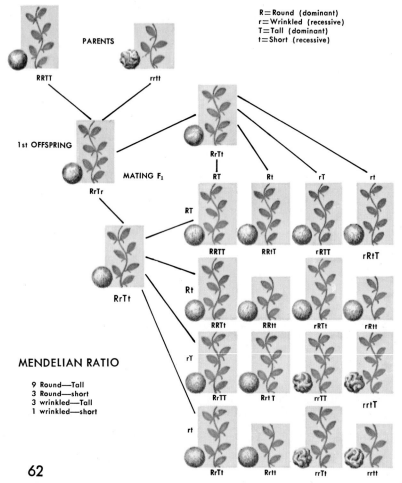

R = Round (dominant)
r = Wrinkled (recessive)
T = Tall (dominant)
t = Short (recessive)

PARENTS

RRTT   rrtt

1st OFFSPRING

RrTr   MATING F₁

RrTr

RrTt

RT

RT   Rt   rT   rt

RrTt

RT   RRTT   RRtT   rRTT   rRtT

Rt   RRTt   RRtt   rRTt   rRtt

rT   RrTT   Rrt T   rrTT   rrtT

rt   RrTt   Rrtt   rrTt   rrtt

MENDELIAN RATIO

9 Round—Tall
3 Round—short
3 wrinkled—Tall
1 wrinkled—short

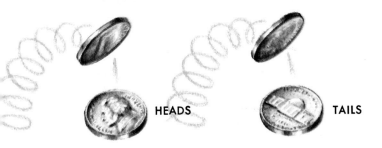

HEADS   TAILS

Probabilities are of major importance in understanding genetic mechanisms. Probability is the likelihood of a particular event happening. If you toss a coin, there is a 50 percent chance that it will come down heads. We can calculate the probability of this. P is the probability, f is the total number of ways in which the event may occur, and u is the number of ways in which some other unfavorable event may occur.

$$P = \frac{f}{f + u}.$$

If we toss a coin 100 times, it is just as likely to come down heads as it is tails for any given throw. So the probability of throwing a head (P_H) will be:

$$P_{Head} = \frac{f(Heads)}{f(Heads) + u(Tails)} = \frac{50}{50 + 50} = \frac{50}{100} = 0.5$$

In genetics, gametes are comparable to the coins, and the zygotes resulting from the union of the gametes are comparable to the heads and tails. In man, with 23 pairs of chromosomes, there are 2^{23} or 8,388,608 different combinations possible in the production of sperms and eggs. Since any one of these sperm may fertilize any of an equal number of kinds of eggs from a female, it is theoretically possible for one pair of humans to produce as many offspring as the world population without any two being identical.

INHERITANCE PROBABILITIES can be calculated just as probabilities are calculated in flipping a coin. With the coin, a value of $P_H = 0.5$ means a 50/50 or a one out of two probability of obtaining a head on any one throw. Similarly, the probability (P_T) of obtaining a tail is also 0.5. The sum of any dependent probabilities is always 1. In the case of the coins, this can be expressed as $P_H + P_T = 1$.

Probabilities range from 0 to 1.0. $P = 1$ implies a particular event is certain to take place. $P = 0$ means an event is impossible. The probability of two or more independent events occurring simultaneously is given by the product of their individual probabilities, or $P = P_1 \times P_2$. In this formula, P is the probability of the events occurring simultaneously, P_1 is the probability of one event, and P_2 is the probability of the other.

Sometimes a single event can have more than one cause. Black color, in guinea pigs below for example, may be produced by all black or by black and white alleles, if black is dominant. Then the probability of such an event (2) that may arise in more than one way is the *sum* of the probabilities for each of its causes (p and q). This can be calculated by $P_2 = P_p + P_q$.

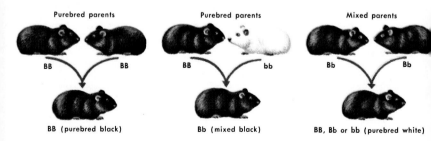

Purebred parents	Purebred parents	Mixed parents
BB BB	BB bb	Bb Bb
BB (purebred black)	Bb (mixed black)	BB, Bb or bb (purebred white)

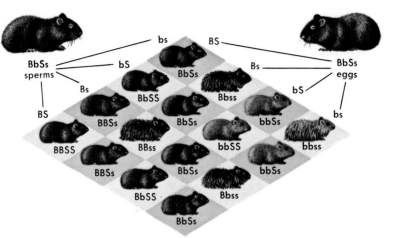

Checkerboard Calculation of Possible Genotypes

CHECKERBOARD shows method for calculating the genotypes in offspring of two guinea pigs that are heterozygous for black, short hair. (B=black, b= brown, S=short hair, and s= long hair.) The four possible gametes from each are arranged along the sides of the checkerboard. Their combinations are plotted in the squares. Since B and S are dominant, a black short phenotype can be produced by BBSS, BbSs, BbSS, and BBSs.

In the combination, there will be 9 black shorts (1 BBSS, 2 BbSs, 4 BbSs, and 2 BBSs), 3 brown shorts (1 bbSS and 2 bbSs), 3 black long (1 BBss and 2 Bbss), and 1 brown long (bbss). This ratio of 9:3:3:1 corresponds to that of the Hardy-Weinberg Principle, below.

ZYGOTES, or fertilized eggs, are formed by two individual gametes, each of which can be regarded as an independent "event." If p is the probability of a zygote with a black chromosome and q is the probability of a zygote with a white chromosome, $p+q=1$.

A zygote with one black and one white chromosome may be produced in two ways—either pq or qp, each giving the identical result. We can calculate the probability of this by random mating in a large population from the formula that gives the product of the male contribution $(p+q)$ and the female contribution $(p+q) \times (p+q) = (p+q)^2 = p^2 + 2pq + q^2 = 1$

This relationship, called the Hardy-Weinberg Principle, shows that in a large, stable population, frequencies of different genotypes are predictable and conservative from one generation to another.

THE MECHANISM OF INHERITANCE revealed by the studies of Mendel and later geneticists showed that each inherited character, such as seed shape or color in peas, is controlled by a pair of genes. One member of each pair (an allele) is contributed by each parent. The genes are located on visible rodlike chromosomes, whose behavior shows a close parallel to that predicted for genes (p. 60). We have already seen how these structures divide in egg and sperm formation and combine in fertilization. But what determines the sex of the new individual?

THE SEX of the offspring is determined by specialized pairs of sex chromosomes. The female parent has one pair of similar chromosomes (X chromosomes, p. 56), and the male parent has one pair of dissimilar chromosomes (X and Y). The division of the chromosomes when eggs and sperms are produced gives the eggs all X chromosomes and the sperm half X and half Y chromosomes. The random pairing in fertilization results in either XX (female) or XY (male).

Other genes, including those that produce hemophilia and some kinds of color blindness, are linked to sex chromosomes. These sex-linked characters can be transmitted to the offspring of apparently "normal" parents.

Sex of animals is determined by the sperm. If it contains a Y chromosome, the offspring will be male.

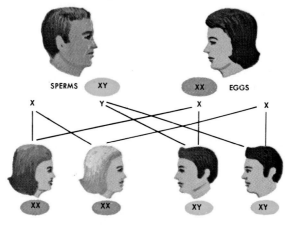

GENES control inheritance, but what controls genes? How do they transmit their complex genetic information from one generation to another?

Chemical analysis of chromosomes has shown that they consist of four basic compounds: two proteins, one with a relatively low molecular weight and the other much higher, plus two nucleic acids, deoxyribonucleic acid (DNA) and ribonucleic acid (RNA). The combination of these four molecules forms *chromatin,* the "stuff" of which chromosomes are made. DNA carries and controls genetic information.

DNA was first suspected to be the "basic component" of genes when it was discovered that the nuclei of both reproductive and body cells of any particular species contained identical amounts of DNA for each chromosome set. One strain of the bacterium *Pneumococcus* could be transformed into another by infecting it with a purified extract from dead cells of the second strain. The "transformed" strain bred true, and the extract was later identified as DNA. This nonliving DNA from a second strain therefore had the ability to transform the hereditary mechanism of bacteria cells. Similar transformations induced in other bacteria show that genes are composed of DNA.

The genetic transformation of *Pneumococcus* Type II cells into Type III cells by the addition of an extract from dead Type III cells.

EXPERIMENTAL CULTURE

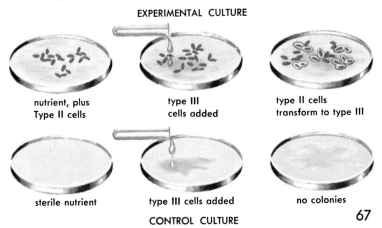

nutrient, plus
Type II cells

type III
cells added

type II cells
transform to type III

sterile nutrient

type III cells added

no colonies

CONTROL CULTURE

67

THE CHEMICAL KEY TO INHERITANCE IS DNA (deoxyribonucleic acid), which controls heredity by regulating instructions of growth and form from cell to cell and from parent to offspring. DNA is present in all living creatures.

In structure, the DNA molecule is a double helix, resembling a ladder that has been repeatedly twisted. Each rung of this molecular ladder is made up of a pair or two from four chemical bases—adenine, thymine, guanine, and cystosine. The size and structure of these bases is such that each "rung pair" always consists of either adenine and thymine or of guanine and cystosine. It is the sequence of the pairs in the rungs that provides the code by which growth instructions are transmitted. From these four basic code substances, an almost infinite variety of sequences can develop.

The portion of a DNA molecular model here shows that each rung of the helix ladder is built of a pair of chemical bases.

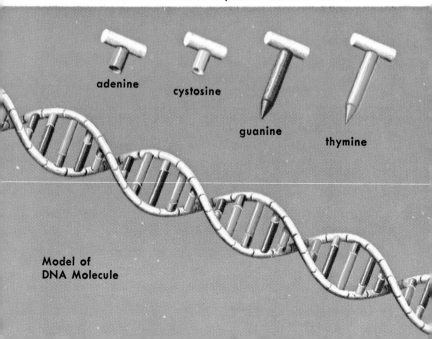

adenine

cystosine

guanine

thymine

Model of
DNA Molecule

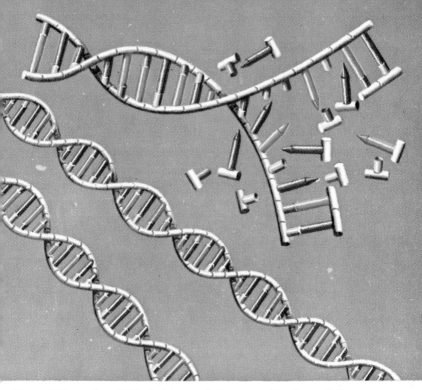

The splitting of a DNA ladder and the recombination of the unzipped rungs with appropriately fitting new base units, identical to their original partners on the rung, produces two new molecules. Half of each new molecule is derived from the original "parent" molecule.

DNA controls growth by having the unique ability to unzip down the middle of the molecular ladder, thus freeing the paired ends of each chemical rung. The exposed compounds then link up with similar new units that are derived from the organism's food supply. As the split of the molecular ladder continues, each half builds an exact replica of itself by this linkage. The rigid sequence of pairing is preserved by the fit of the original structure. In this way the DNA molecule can reproduce itself over and over again.

PROTEIN MANUFACTURE. RNA (ribonucleic acid) has a structure much like that of DNA. Unlike DNA, however, it is not confined to the cell nucleus. It is the essential messenger in the manufacture of proteins by cells. Proteins are involved in every body process. They form the basic material of living organisms. They are very large molecules, made up of various combinations of 20 essential kinds of amino acids.

RNA is manufactured from DNA, from which it differs in having one more oxygen atom in its sugar (ribose) and in having uracil instead of thymine in the molecular structure. Slightly different "messenger" RNA molecules control the manufacture of each of the many kinds of protein. Each is imprinted with a coded template of its structure. Selected amino acids are then tagged by still other distinctive "transfer" RNA molecules, each imprinted with a structure that enables it to bring the particular amino acid to the messenger template. When these amino acids are arranged and combined in correct sequence, RNA may separate from newly produced protein and perform its task again.

The messenger RNA bar carries the code, while each of three smaller components of the RNA unit is structured to accept a particular amino acid shape. In the background is a DNA helix.

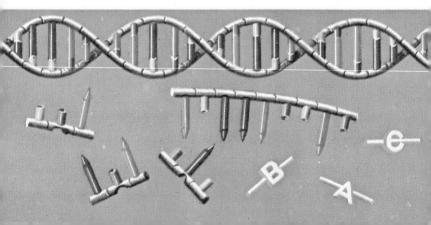

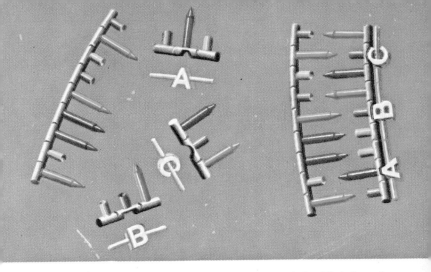

Transfer RNA units locate (Left) and transport their (Right) various amino acids toward the coded RNA template bar.

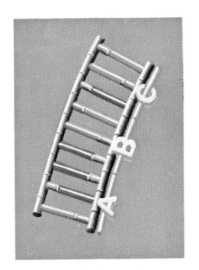

Transfer RNA units unite with a messenger unit opposite their paired partner compounds, so arranged as to build an amino acid sequence into a particular protein molecule.

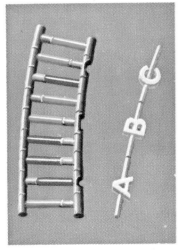

The new protein molecule constructed from a sequence of amino acids, separates from the RNA. Most proteins consist of hundreds of amino acid units that are arranged together.

WHAT ARE THE SOURCES OF VARIABILITY? If genetic equilibrium in any population is so conservative, how does change ever take place? How could evolution in plants and animals occur? What are the sources of variations in plants and animals?

No two individuals are ever exactly alike. These individual differences are as recognizable in dogs or in goldfish as they are in man. Some differences are acquired during life through behavior or from the environment. Dieting, or lack of it, influences weight. Respiratory diseases may be produced by smoking or by living in a polluted atmosphere. But many individual characteristics are hereditary, not environmental. These include such physical features as eye color, complexion, color blindness, and height. How do these differences arise?

Variations of this kind are produced in two ways: by a shuffling and redistribution of genes during reproduction (recombination) and by spontaneous changes in gene structure leading to new characteristics (mutation).

Crowd scene illustrates variability of our own species.

RECOMBINATION is the chief source of variation. It may occur either by a simple recombination of the chromosomes when fertilization between parents takes place or by a crossing-over that involves an exchange of genetic material between chromosomes. Recombination involves the formation of new genotypes by the reshuffling of existing ones (p. 64). In organisms that reproduce asexually, much less potential variation is possible than in those that reproduce sexually. This has put an evolutionary "premium" on sexual reproduction. Sexual reproduction is the major source of the wide variation in plant and animal species.

CROSSING-OVER of chromosomes sometimes takes place during meiosis, the formation of sex cells. This results from chromosome strands sticking together so that an exchange of genes takes place between chromosome pairs. Where these chromosomes are joined and the exchanges occur are called *chiasmata*. Each cross-over doubles the number of kinds of gametes and modifies the linkage of genes, thus providing an important source of variability. In the illustration of crossing-over below, different colors represent different genes.

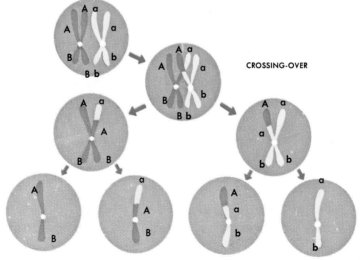

CROSSING-OVER

Horned Hereford   Polled Hereford

Polled Hereford cattle lack horns because of the effects of mutation of a gene which regulates horn secretion.

MUTATIONS are changes in genetic material that produce new characteristics. The change may be obvious (as examples, wing form in flies, hornless polled Hereford cattle, short-legged Ancon sheep, or double flowers), or it may be an inconspicuous and subtle chemical and physiological difference. Particular genes may mutate in more than one way, and many can reverse the direction of change. Each gene has a distinctive mutation rate. Some will mutate only once per million gametes, for example, while others undergo mutations more than 500 times as frequently. The rate of mutation can be influenced by various factors, such as temperature changes, radiation, and chemical stimulants. Conspicuous mutations are more often harmful to the organism than are the smaller ones.

Mutation seems to be caused by slight imperfections in the self-copying chemical structures of the DNA molecules that make up the genes. They may affect the number and structures of the DNA molecules of the genes. They may also affect the number and structure of chromosomes. Occasionally the chromosomes divide but the cell does not, resulting in a whole new set of chromosomes (polyploidy). The new mutants breed true and do not revert to the original type.

GENETIC DRIFT was discovered by the American geneticist Sewall Wright, who studied the mathematics of population genetics. The gene pool—that is, the total gene contribution of a particular population to its offspring—is greatly influenced by the size of the population. In very small populations, such as those isolated from their parent group, chance plays relatively a much greater role in producing genetic change, sometimes leading to non-adaptive changes. Although the reality of genetic drift has been confirmed in laboratory experiments, its role in evolution is still not clear. It may be of some importance in small populations that later increase in size and may account for some of the puzzling, persistent non-adaptive or neutral changes observed in diversified wild populations.

Variability thus arises from four possible sources—recombination, crossing-over, mutation, and genetic drift. Of these, recombination is by far the most important. Once it was thought that variability alone could produce evolutionary change, without aid from additional factors. Statistical analysis showed, however, that only natural selection could account for the perpetuation and refinement of the endless adaptations shown by living things. Variability is not the whole of the evolutionary recipe, but it is the essential raw material on which everything else depends.

Small isolated population may be most influenced by genetic drift.

ISOLATION of gene pools distinguishes species from races and demes, which are populations capable of interbreeding when they come into contact. The development of isolation between once interbreeding groups is an important factor in evolution. Once isolated, each population will undergo independent, gradual genetic change until it is no longer compatible with the group with which it once interbred. Since climatic and ecologic conditions undergo slow changes, there is a dynamic interaction between them and species distribution. Many now-divided ranges of species reflect isolation of originally widespread populations.

Isolation may arise in different ways. It may be geographic, as in some island populations (p. 19). Related species that do not overlap in territory are called allopatric; those that do, sympatric. Genetic isolation may arise between either kind of population. It may involve ecological, behavioral, morphological, or physiological differences, any of which may prevent mating. Even if mating does take place, various internal cellular or developmental barriers may prevent fertilization or produce nonviable, weak or sterile hybrids.

GEOGRAPHIC ISOLATION is shown below in schematic form: (A) widespread species with no geographic variation, (B) different populations develop in extremes of ranges, (C) partial geographic barrier develops, (D) barrier becomes a total preventative to interbreeding of two populations, (E) cumulative genetic differences become so great that genetic separation produces two species, even if the barrier is eliminated.

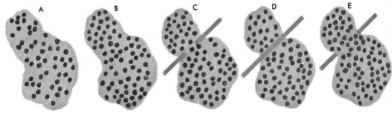

MIGRATION of populations into new areas may lead to permanent colonization. In some cases, different areas may have very closely similar climates and terrains but be separated by such barriers as oceans, deserts, or mountains. Over long periods, a few individuals may cross these barriers and become established in their new environment. The new colony will interbreed in isolation from the parent population and may in time develop into a new species.

Some of the greatest transformations in the history of life have arisen by migration. These include the colonization of the land by plants and animals.

INTERCONTINENTAL MIGRATION of some Pleistocene mammals is shown here. Asia and North America were periodically joined by the Bering Straits. The "filter" effect of these island connections confined some mammals (circled) to their original continents. (After Kay and Colbert.)

Camel

Raccoon

Mammoth

Mastodon

Puma

Horse

Bison

Pig

Horse

Rhinoceros

Peccary

Glyptodont

Pronghorn

Porcupine

Sloth

NATURAL SELECTION is the second major component of the evolutionary process. Left to themselves, large and randomly interbreeding populations will move toward genetic equilibrium (p. 65). Natural selection is the net result of all the physical and biological environmental factors that tend to disturb this equilibrium and change a population's gene pool. Natural selection does not itself create new variations; it selects, winnows, and preserves existing variations. The genetic components of a population determine what it may become; selection determines what it will become. Inheritance provides it with its potential; selection transforms potential to actuality.

THE ACTION of natural selection depends on the tendency of all species to produce more offspring than can normally survive (p. 24) in an environment of limited capacity. Better adapted organisms will live longer than the less well adapted, hence produce a greater number of descendants. The descendant population will include an increasingly large proportion of individuals that have inherited favorable features from their parents.

Natural selection is rarely a "struggle for existence" between two competing individuals. Predation and direct competition are only two of many factors involved, including such other things as mobility, physiological and structural efficiency, resistance to disease, and sexual vigor.

Natural selection produces differential reproduction. It is the "survival of the fittest" only in the sense that the fittest produce more offspring. In effect, it not only eliminates the less well adapted characteristics but also produces positive results.

Strong bull—many offspring

Weak bull—no offspring

SELECTION PRESSURE varies from season to season and from place to place. It is influenced by such fluctuating factors as climate, population size, food supply, and migration. Selection generally does not lead to long-term stability because so many of these and other factors undergo more or less continuous change and are reinforced by such major changes as colonization of a new environment, isolation, or change in the existing geography of an area.

Natural selection does not operate as a steam-roller effect on one character, but as a subtle series of interacting "compromises" that affect the whole organism and may influence many different characteristics. Selection is a cumulative process. Even over a short period, its effects can be substantial (p. 84). Over long periods its effects can be enormous.

The increasing adaptation of a population to its environment is the result of natural selection. Each niche is generally filled by only a single species, but a number of species may share the same area by their various adaptations to specific food supplies or to habitats. The better adapted leave more offspring, gradually changing the character of the descendant population.

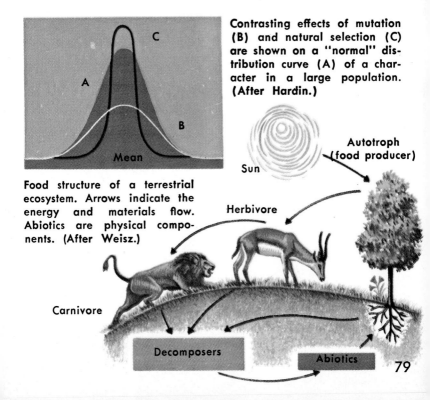

Contrasting effects of mutation (B) and natural selection (C) are shown on a "normal" distribution curve (A) of a character in a large population. (After Hardin.)

Food structure of a terrestrial ecosystem. Arrows indicate the energy and materials flow. Abiotics are physical components. (After Weisz.)

C

A

B

Mean

Sun

Autotroph (food producer)

Herbivore

Carnivore

Decomposers

Abiotics

79

PROOF OF NATURAL SELECTION came long after Darwin presented the theory in *The Origin of Species*. Darwin compared it with artificial domestic selection and demonstrated its probable causes and apparent effects, but the process itself had not been demonstrated. Many laboratory studies have since been conducted that illustrate both the operation and the effects of natural selection. In these, the biologist attempts to duplicate and to isolate certain natural environments and to analyze their interacting processes.

IN MICE and other wild animals, color changes are often closely associated with the predominant color of the background soil and vegetation where the animals live. In Florida, for example, the deer mouse (*Peromyscus maniculatus*) shows a continuous color transition from very light on the coral sand of island reefs to dark in inland areas of darker soil.

Is this the result of natural selection?

Researchers worked with two color varieties—gray and buff. Two contrasting backgrounds were set up in a large darkened cage. The soil in the cages more or less matched the color of each of the shades of mice.

Eight mice, four of each color, were exposed to a barn owl for 15 minutes. The backgrounds were alternated with each experiment. After 88 "experiments," it was found that the owl had taken 107 of the "non-matching" mice and only 62 of the better concealed ones. This shows how powerful a selective factor protective background coloration can be, even over a short period.

62 Matching

107 Non-matching

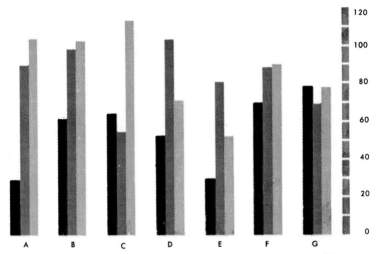

Viability of seven strains (A-G) of homozygous *Drosophila* fruit flies with deleterious genes, before and after the experiment described below. The viability is shown as % of normal viability (100%). Black columns indicate the viability before the experiment; the red columns, viability of untreated stocks after 50 generations; the yellow columns, of stocks irradiated with X-rays after 50 generations. (After Dobzhansky and Spassky.)

POORLY ADAPTED ANIMALS are rarely found in nature, but the effect of natural selection upon such poorly adapted forms can be observed under experimental conditions. Dobzhansky and Spassky raised samples of the fruit fly *Drosophila* that were homozygous for seven different chromosome combinations (A-G). Each was associated with some abnormality such as retarded development or deformed wings, legs, and abdomens—that resulted in a low viability.

Each of these stocks was raised for fifty generations and kept in crowded culture bottles to increase selection pressure.

The populations were sampled at regular intervals to study the chromosomes of representative individuals. In most cases, there was a rapid and marked decline in the abundance of the deleterious combinations. The experiment included exposure of one sample of each stock to X-ray radiation, but these produced no significant differences.

Of the 14 stocks, 11 showed marked increase in viability, 2 declined in viability, and 1 remained unchanged. Of the control groups, unmixed with the stronger natural populations, 8 showed a marked deterioration, 6 were unchanged or showed only slight improvements.

NATURAL POPULATIONS are also studied to determine the effects of natural selection. One example is how natural selection might have produced the differences that exist between the various kinds of Darwin's finches on the Galapagos Islands (p. 18). Typical finches, such as sparrows and cardinals, have strong conical beaks that are used to crush seeds. But the Galapagos finches show a great variety of beaks. Some are stout and conical, others slender, and still others adapted for quite different diets.

This diversity was probably produced by the presence of many vacant ecological niches when the finches first became established on the Galapagos.

Increasing numbers of birds feeding on a limited seed supply provided the selective pressure that favored those that could exist on new food.

DARWIN'S FINCHES (GALAPAGOS ISLANDS)

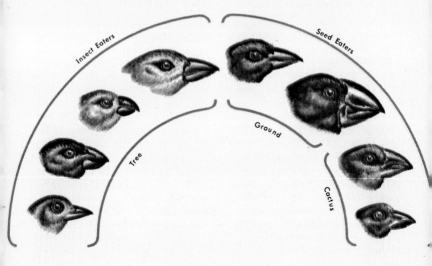

Insect Eaters

Seed Eaters

Tree

Ground

Cactus

The ground-loving finches retained their seed-eating habits, although individual species show marked variation in beak proportions that seem related to particular types of seed preferences. Other finches turned to kinds of food and habits that are characteristic of species of other families on the continents. Some became tree-dwellers, including types that are warblerlike insectivores and others that are parrotlike vegetarians. Still others became specialized for feeding on cacti. An insectivore developed a strong beak that it uses to bore into bark. Lacking the long tongue of true woodpeckers (p. 42), it uses a cactus spine to extract the insects from the burrows.

All finches are rather similar in their general size and have dull plumage, probably because of the dark volcanic rocks that outcrop over much of their territory.

The Galapagos finches probably arose from an ancestral South American form, but they now differ so greatly from all existing mainland finches that their ancestry cannot be recognized. This marked difference suggests that the finches reached the islands earlier than other species, which are much closer to the mainland forms. The ancestral finches presumably reached the islands by being "accidentally" carried there, perhaps aided by oceanic currents. It seems most unlikely that the Galapagos Islands were ever joined to the mainland.

In contrast to the diversity of the Galapagos finches, David Lack has shown that in the neighboring Cocos Island there is only a single species of finch, although the island provides varied habitats and lacks many other typical species of continental birds. This seems to result from the single island of Cocos lacking the numbers of small, isolated environments that are provided by the archipelago nature of the Galapagos Islands. (See map p. 19)

Tool-using Finch
(Amarhnynchus pallidus)

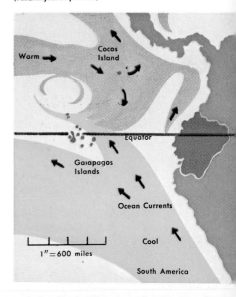

Warm →

Cocos Island

Equator

Galapagos Islands

Ocean Currents

Cool

South America

1" = 600 miles

NATURAL SELECTION IN ACTION is shown by the peppered moth (p. 47), which is an example of a species that has shown a striking change in the frequency of a dark (melanic) form in the last century.

This moth was well known to the many amateur entomologists in Britain in the early years of the 19th century. Until 1845, it was known only in the "peppered" form, which has dark markings on a light wing background. In that year, a dark form was discovered in the industrial city of Manchester. At that time the dark form made up less than 1 percent of the total population. Within fifty years it made up 99 percent of the population in the Manchester area. The black moth is now the predominant form over much of England, and the original peppered form is abundant only in non-industrial areas where pollution has not blackened the trees on which the moth lives. In some of the non-industrial eastern areas of the country where heavy smog is carried in, the black form also dominates the moth population.

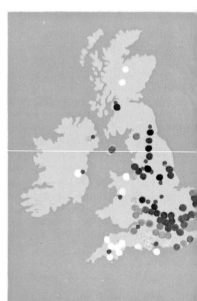

Recent studies in Manchester and other industrial cities where stringent anti-pollution ordinances have been enforced, have shown a reversal of the trend towards darker forms, and a slow but marked increase in abundance of the lighter peppered forms.

PEPPERED MOTH DISTRIBUTION
IN BRITAIN
- (red) Major industrial cities
- o (white) light form predominant
- (black) dark form predominant
- (gray) intermediate population

Industrial Area

Agricultural Area

INDUSTRIAL MELANISM (the predominance of dark varieties) is also shown by about 70 other species of moths in Europe. In the United States, the Pittsburgh region shows a comparable predominance of once rare black forms in almost 100 species of moths.

The cause of industrial melanism lies in the interaction of a dominant gene, producing the black mutation, and natural selection. H. B. D. Kettlewell has demonstrated the importance of natural selection by studying rates of bird predation on the two forms of the peppered moth. He released known numbers of marked moths of each form in two areas and analyzed the number of each form that he recaptured by attracting them to a light at night. In the industrial Birmingham area, where the local population has 90 percent black forms, he released 477 black and 137 light individuals. He recaptured 40 percent of the black forms but only 19 percent of the peppered.

In the unpolluted coastal area of Dorset, from almost 1,000 of the two colors of moths released, 6 percent of the black and 12.5 percent of the light forms were recaptured. So in polluted areas, the black-white recapture ratio was 2:1. In unpolluted areas it was exactly reversed—1:2.

In both areas, careful observation and filming of birds eating the moths from tree trunks confirmed that these ratios were the results of relative predation.

FOSSILS also demonstrate the effects of natural selection. B. Kurten has shown its effects in the European cave bear *(Ursus spelaeus)* that inhabited northern Europe during the Pleistocene. Kurten collected fossils from caves in the Odessa region of the U.S.S.R. By comparing these with skeletons of the closely related living bear *(Ursus arctos)*, he was able to divide each of the fossil populations into growth stages. The fossils from all localities showed strong separation into similar, yearly growth stages, probably because the caves in which they were collected were inhabited only during annual "hibernation." The analysis of these growth stages demonstrates the effects of natural selection.

YOUNGEST STAGES of the cave bear equal in size to newborn cubs of living bears are rare, probably because of the fragility of the bones. The most abundant growth stage has all the permanent teeth developed, equivalent to about 4 or 5 months in living bears, suggesting birth during the period of winter dormancy, but a high mortality of cubs toward the end of this time. The next growth stage is 1.4 years, indicating the next annual "hibernation." At 4 years, bears were fully grown. Life expectation at birth was about 3.5 years; maximum age, 18 years. Dividing the total number of individuals in a given age group by the sum of these and all older individuals gives the mortality index for the group.

Pleistocene Cave bear

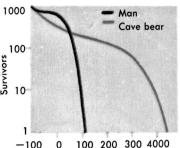

Survivorship curves from birth for cave bears and man, showing the similarity of the curves. (After Kurten.)

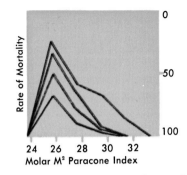

Selection pressure on form of paracone of second molar teeth of cave bear is indicated by reduction of variation and development of a relatively smaller paracone with increasing age. (After Kurten.)

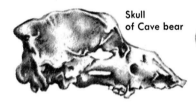

Skull of Cave bear

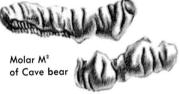

Molar M² of Cave bear

TEETH of fossil cave bears are very sensitive to natural selection, because survival depends on successful feeding prior to hibernation. Kurten studied the form of the second molar teeth (M²). The ratio 100x the length of the largest cusp (paracone) to the total length of the second molar showed a significant change, becoming smaller with increasing age. The younger age groups were far more variable than the older, but forms with less well-adapted teeth were eliminated.

Older tooth measurements gave comparable results. Samples from other caves gave similar but not identical results, suggesting differences in selective pressure between different local environmental niches in which the bears lived.

87

ADAPTATION is the continuing result of natural selection. Many organisms are very precisely adapted to particular niches or to particular ways of life. The birds of Hawaii provide a classic illustration of how an ancestral group becomes adapted to special niches in a new environment. Hawaii consists of a group of isolated volcanic islands situated in the mid-Pacific. Like most oceanic islands, the number of land birds is small. The high degree of specialization of some of the birds makes them vulnerable to environmental change.

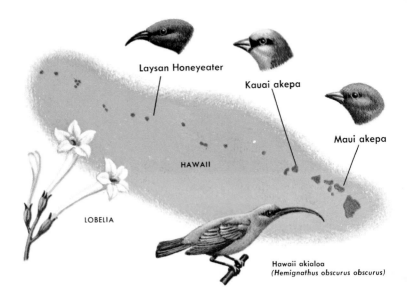

Laysan Honeyeater

Kauai akepa

Maui akepa

HAWAII

LOBELIA

Hawaii akialoa
(Hemignathus obscurus obscurus)

SICKLEBILLS, or drepanidids, are a family of birds found only in Hawaii. Like Darwin's finches in the Galapagos Islands (p. 83), they have adapted themselves to a wide diversity of conditions. The original forms seem to have fed on the insects and nectar of shortbelled flowers. They probably had short, slender beaks. Other forms show diversity of adaptations to different diets, including some with remarkably long, curved beaks for feeding on the long, tubular flowers of the Hawaiian lobelia. Some of the various forms of sicklebills are illustrated. Nine of the 22 known species are now extinct.

Pseudonestor

Psittirostra kona

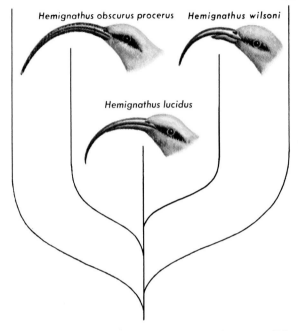
Hemignathus obscurus procerus   Hemignathus wilsoni

Hemignathus lucidus

Probable evolution of one group of drepanidids from an ancestor, possibly similar to the Honeyeater (p. 88) is shown above. Drepanidid beaks show adaption to various diets. *Hemignathus obscurus* uses its elongated beak chiefly to probe for insects in bark cavities, although other species use their long "sickle-bills" chiefly to probe lobelia flowers for nectar. The now extinct *H. lucidus* had a short lower mandible, which is reduced even further in *H. wilsoni,* which uses it, woodpecker-fashion, as a chisel. The long tubular tongues of insect-eating species reflect their development from nectar-feeding forms. *Pseudonestor* has a parrot like bill, while seed-eating species, such as *Psittirostra kona,* have heavy finch-like beaks.

MIMICRY is relatively common in insects and in some flowers. In insects it seems to have arisen chiefly for defense; in flowers, for pollination. The influence of natural selection in the development of mimicry is shown by the distribution of mimic species only in areas where their models are common. Where the models are abundant, the mimics show greater variability, which can be explained only by assuming that the lower predator familiarity with the models in such areas has produced lower selection pressure on the mimics. Development of mimics depends not on "accidental" parallel mutations but on a series of interacting genes that have undergone strong selection.

THE SLIPPER ORCHID of Europe and the Middle East emits a perfume that attracts a wasp which pollinates it. Other related *Ophrys* orchids have bright, insectlike flowers that aid in attracting male wasps.

INSECTS have developed various protective shapes and colors. The harmless bumblebee moth, for example, is a mimic of the stinging bumblebee. The treehoppers below look like thorns.

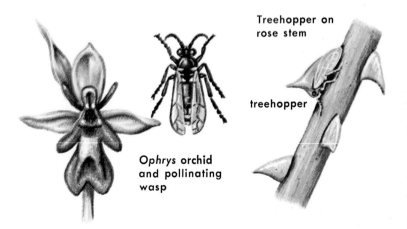

Ophrys orchid and pollinating wasp

Treehopper on rose stem

treehopper

SEXUAL SELECTION is the sum of various characters by which one partner, generally the male, of a species attracts a mate and repels rivals of the same sex. Since it increases the individual's reproductive productivity, it constitutes a distinct kind of selection. Elaborate male plumage and song in birds, courtship displays, more intense male coloration, greater size and antlers in various animals—these are some of the characteristics that may result. The relative importance of sexual selection as a component of natural selection is still not clear. Darwin was convinced it was of major importance, but subsequent writers have been less sure.

MALE SUPERB LYREBIRD of Australia stands with its elaborate tail feathers extended and quivering, as it performs its courtship display. The female resembles the male in color but lacks the specialized tail feathers. Young male birds are like the females. They do not develop the tail feathers until they are about three years old.

Each male establishes a large territory, and throughout this area, he builds a series of mounds of earth, each about a yard in diameter. He patrols his territory by visiting each mound and performing his display on it. The display begins with a vocal performance that includes a series of mimicking sounds and calls.

NATURAL SELECTION IN MAN is reduced in its obvious effects by the structures of society and by the elaborate patterns of family care. Even so, many body features show the influence of natural selection. Some gene changes also demonstrate its effects. Sickle-cell anemia, a disease caused by a single gene, is marked by distortion of the blood cells from their normal disc shape to sickle shape which blocks the flow of blood in capillaries and thus causes anemia. Sometimes death results when sufferers are short of breath or work at high altitudes. In West and Central Africa, where malaria is endemic, populations with a sickle-gene equilibrium frequency of up to 20 percent are common. Among descendants of these people in the United States, frequency of sickle-cell anemia has dropped to 9 percent in two centuries. How has this come about?

The frequency of a sickle-cell gene in Africa is plotted below as percent of population. High frequencies are restricted to equatorial areas in which tertian malaria is an important cause of death. North and south of this belt, malaria is less common and is benign. Similar high frequencies occur in malarial areas of Sicily, Greece, Turkey, and India. (After Allison.)

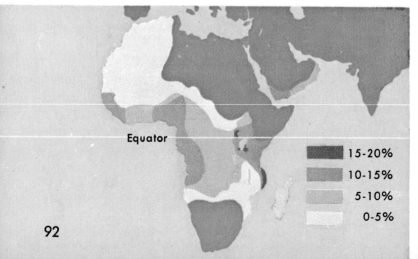

Equator

15-20%
10-15%
5-10%
0-5%

THE SICKLE GENE was demonstrated by biologist Vernon Ingram to have the ability to change one of the three hundred amino acid units in the hemoglobin molecules that make up the red blood cells. At one point in the chain of nineteen different amino acids that make up the protein, valine is substituted for glutamic acid. The result is that normal red blood corpuscles become sickle-shaped.

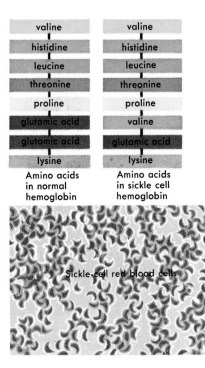

valine	valine
histidine	histidine
leucine	leucine
threonine	threonine
proline	proline
glutamic acid	valine
glutamic acid	glutamic acid
lysine	lysine

Amino acids in normal hemoglobin

Amino acids in sickle cell hemoglobin

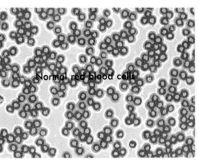

Normal red blood cells

Sickle-cell red blood cells

HETEROZYGOUS sickle genes have comparatively little adverse effect under normal conditions, but the homozygous condition has far more serious effects, often causing blood clotting or premature death.

Why do sickle genes still persist if natural selection is effective? It so happens that sickle-shaped hemoglobin is resistant to infection by the malarial parasite *Plasmodium,* which feeds on red blood cells. In malarial areas, therefore, a selective equilibrium exists, with the heterozygous sickle-cell individuals resistant and thus favored. The homozygous individuals (with 2 sickle-cell genes) often die. An equilibrium tends to occur between the number of people with no sickle-cell gene (these are the "normal" individuals) who die of malaria and those with two sickle-cell genes who die of anemia or blood clotting. In this case, an apparently harmful genetic effect may be preserved because of side benefits. In malaria-free U. S., the condition has no survival value.

Thus, natural selection represents not a blind, crushing wave of extinction but the resolution of conflicting environmental demands on a population. It involves subtle interplay of internal and external influences.

MISSING LINKS (p. 52) confirm the action of natural selection and demonstrate the way in which it operates. Once it was argued that natural selection could not possibly have produced the elaborate complex of changes required to bring about such major evolutionary changes as the development of amphibians from fish or birds from reptiles. Transitional fossil forms, or "missing links," show how the process took place.

A Devonian lobefin crossopterygian fish climbs ashore.

Labyrinthodont amphibian, a descendant, goes ashore clumsily.

RANDOM NATURAL SELECTION, the critics once argued, could not have produced the elaborate series of variations that gradually transformed reptilian arms into bird wings and gave birds a light and modified skeleton, feathers, and similar features. Each of these endless minor modifications, it was thought, might offer no special advantage—not enough to bring about the various supposedly interdependent and coordinated changes that were involved.

But *Archaeopteryx* and other transitional fossil forms (pp. 52-53) show that change from one major group to another was a piecemeal process. There was not one big jump or a synchronized development of all the various characters involved. In *Archaeopteryx,* some features, such as the brain, claws, teeth, and sternum, were primitive and reptilian; others, such as wings and feathers and the general body shape, were already fully birdlike. This jumbled mosaic-evolution is exactly what we should expect if natural selection has been an effective agent of change.

MOSAIC EVOLUTION is shown well in the ichthyostegids, primitive amphibians of the Devonian (p. 98). They had many fishlike features. The chart gives a breakdown of their amphibian versus fishlike characteristics, with 100 points for fully developed amphibian form and 0 for fully fishlike form.

Score	Character
0	Vertebrae—form of
0	Tail structure
75	Skull structure
75	Eyes—position of
100	Limbs
100	Shoulder and hip girdles
100	Skull articulation
100	Ribs—form of

Ichthyostega, a primitive Devonian amphibian from East Greenland. About 3 feet long. A reconstruction.

Skeleton of *Ichthyostega* probably resembles closely that of the ancestors from which amphibians evolved.

Diplovertebron, a labyrinthodont amphibian of the Carboniferous, with many resemblances to the ichthyostegids.

Eusthenopteron, a Devonian lobefin crossopterygian fish 2 feet long, has many resemblances to the ichthyostegids.

95

TIME is the final component of the evolutionary recipe. Early opponents of evolution contended that the age of the earth, then regarded as less than 40 million years, did not allow enough time for the slow process of change that evolution involved. These estimates were based on the rate of cooling of a supposedly once molten earth. But the development of other methods of dating suggested a much greater age, and the use of radioactivity now indicates that the earth is probably about 5 billion years old. This is ample time for evolution to have taken place. The development of a geologic time scale puts the fossil record into perspective, and reveals the order and sequence of the various forms of life.

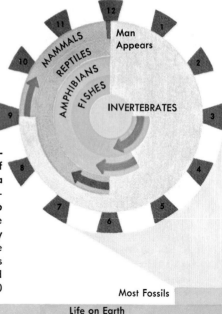

THE GEOLOGIC CLOCK

Shows last 600 million years of earth's history, each hour representing 50 million years.

Man Appears

MAMMALS
REPTILES
AMPHIBIANS
FISHES
INVERTEBRATES

Most Fossils

Life on Earth

Age of Earth—about 5 billion years

ANALOGIES help us to appreciate the enormous interval of time this represents. Suppose a cosmic historian writing a history of the earth began to write at the creation of the earth and wrote one line every thousand years. If the books he produced were the size of this one you are reading, he would by now have produced 94,000 books.

RADIOACTIVE ELEMENTS, such as uranium and radium, have unstable atomic nuclei that undergo spontaneous breakdown at a constant, measurable rate to form other, more stable elements. Uranium, for example, produces a series of "daughter" elements and finally yields lead and helium. One gram of uranium produces 1/7000 grams of lead every million years. This rate is unaffected by any changes in heat or pressure. Measurement of the ratio of "old" uranium to "new" lead in uranium minerals provides an indication of the age of the rocks in which they are found.

Other radioactive elements used in age measurements include lead-thorium, potassium-argon, rubidium-strontium, and carbon. Studies of meteorites, which seem to be "left over" fragments from the development of the solar system, and the rate of expansion of the universe tend to confirm a figure of about 4.5-5.0 billion years for the age of the earth.

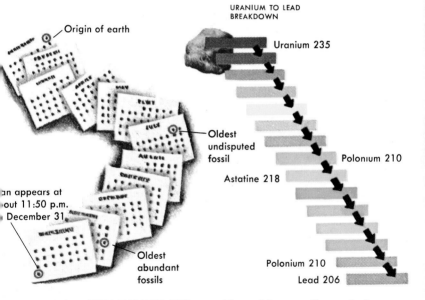

URANIUM TO LEAD BREAKDOWN

Uranium 235

Polonium 210

Astatine 218

Polonium 210

Lead 206

Origin of earth

Oldest undisputed fossil

Man appears at about 11:50 p.m. December 31

Oldest abundant fossils

SCALING DOWN EARTH'S HISTORY into a model single calendar year with the origin of the earth on January 1st and the present day on December 31st would make each second equivalent to 167 years and each minute to 10,000 years.

The oldest undisputed fossils would appear about July 1; the oldest abundant fossils, about November 18. Man would appear at about 11:50 p.m. on December 31. All recorded history would fall in the final 40 seconds of the year.

97

| ERAS | MILLIONS | | PERIOD | THE GEOLOGIC TIME SCALE |
	YEARS AGO	DU-RATION		
CENOZOIC	2	2	QUATERNARY	
	63	62	TERTIARY	
MESOZOIC			CRETACEOUS	
	136	71		
			JURASSIC	
	190	54		
	225	35	TRIASSIC	
PALEOZOIC			PERMIAN	
	280	55		
	325	45	PENNSYLVANIAN	
	345	20	MISSISSIPPIAN	
			DEVONIAN	
	395	50		
	430	35	SILURIAN	
			ORDOVICIAN	
	500	70		
			CAMBRIAN	
	570	70		
PRE-CAMBRIAN	4,030		PRECAMBRIAN	

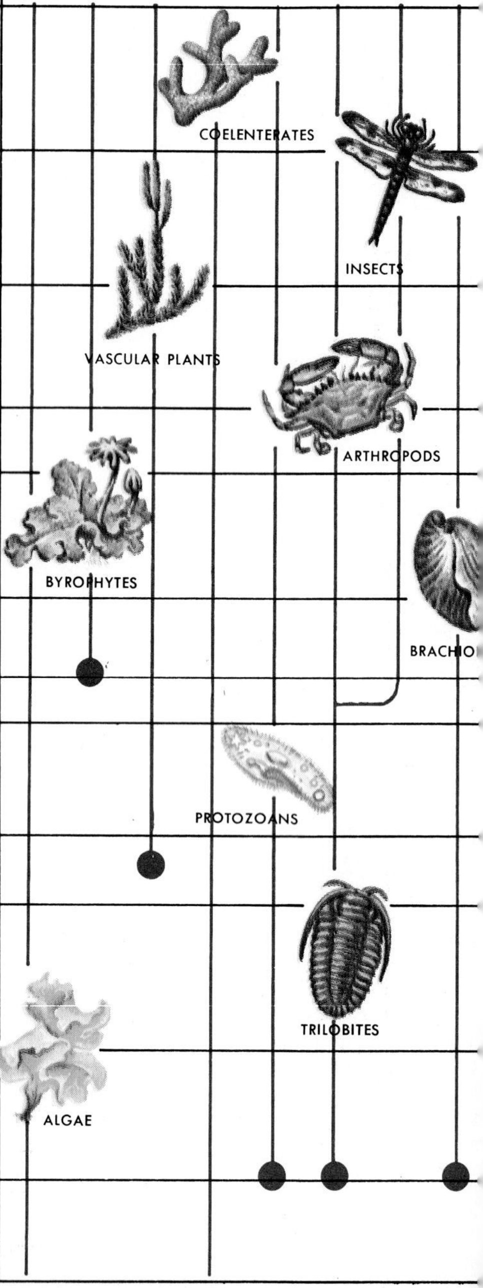

COELENTERATES

INSECTS

VASCULAR PLANTS

ARTHROPODS

BYROPHYTES

BRACHIO

PROTOZOANS

TRILOBITES

ALGAE

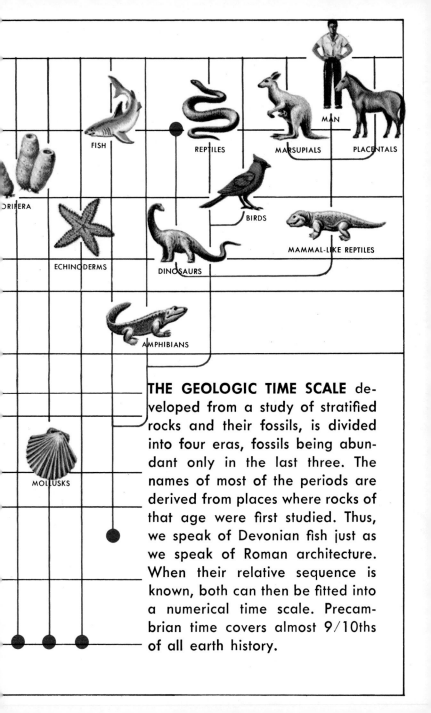

FISH

REPTILES

MARSUPIALS

MAN

PLACENTALS

PORIFERA

BIRDS

MAMMAL-LIKE REPTILES

ECHINODERMS

DINOSAURS

AMPHIBIANS

MOLLUSKS

THE GEOLOGIC TIME SCALE developed from a study of stratified rocks and their fossils, is divided into four eras, fossils being abundant only in the last three. The names of most of the periods are derived from places where rocks of that age were first studied. Thus, we speak of Devonian fish just as we speak of Roman architecture. When their relative sequence is known, both can then be fitted into a numerical time scale. Precambrian time covers almost 9/10ths of all earth history.

RATES OF EVOLUTION vary enormously from one species to another. The small brachipod *Lingula,* an inhabitant of warm, shallow seas, has scarcely changed in the last 400 million years. But the spectacular diversification of mammals has taken place within the last 60 million years. Development of a geologic time scale allows us to analyze and interpret these differing rates, which may be expressed in various ways.

IN STRUCTURES, rates of change can be measured for some fossil groups. In the evolution of early Tertiary horses, changes in dimensions of molar teeth were only 0.15 mm per million years. This is about equal to the diameter of a human hair. Single populations often contained up to twenty times as much variation in tooth dimensions. Such slow transformation can be observed only in fossils.

TRANSFORMATION OF SPECIES from one into another for Tertiary mammals (p. 132) has been calculated to be about 500,000 years. With such slow rates, it is not surprising that few examples of the development of new species can be observed in living populations. Such rates also allow ample time for the operation of "slow" evolutionary mechanisms, such as the selection of small variations.

PLEISTOCENE
PLIOCENE
MIOCENE
OLIGOCENE
EOCENE
PALEOCENE

ECOLOGICAL REPLACEMENT of some extinct groups by others of similar environmental habits suggests that competition between the two groups may have been a factor in some cases of extinction. The width of each column in the diagram is proportional to the diversity of the group.

RAPID DIVERSIFICATION of Miocene horses from browsing to grazing corresponded to the widespread change from lowland forests to upland prairies in North America and the first appearance of fossil grasses. This interaction seems to confirm the importance of natural selection (p. 101).

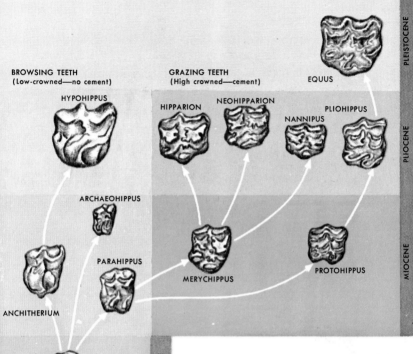

BROWSING TEETH
(Low-crowned—no cement)

HYPOHIPPUS

GRAZING TEETH
(High crowned—cement)

EQUUS

HIPPARION   NEOHIPPARION   PLIOHIPPUS

NANNIPUS

ARCHAEOHIPPUS

PARAHIPPUS

MERYCHIPPUS

PROTOHIPPUS

ANCHITHERIUM

MESOHIPPUS

EPIHIPPUS

EOHIPPUS

PLEISTOCENE

PLIOCENE

MIOCENE

OLIGOCENE

EOCENE

EVOLUTION OF HORSES
(Teeth drawn to scale—After Simpson)

PATTERNS OF CHANGE become evident in some groups when the time factor is considered. The rapid diversification of horses in Miocene times represented a change in feeding habit from browsing to grazing, corresponding to the widespread change from lowland forests to upland prairies in North America and the first appearance of fossil grasses. This seems to be an interaction confirming the importance of natural selection (p. 51).

A RECIPE FOR EVOLUTION showing the interplay of the various factors involved, can be summed up for any population as demonstrated in the diagram below. Such a simple recipe does not mean that evolution is itself simple or that it follows a clearly predictable pattern. The reverse is the case. The interaction of these various processes produces an enormously complex dynamic system. Both the complexity and the potentiality for novelty of the evolutionary process are indicated by the great diversity of living things.

VARIATION:

Genetic Recombination

+

NATURAL SELECTION:

Over-Production Limited Food Supply

+

TIME

→

ISOLATION:

Geographical: Genetic

↓

GENETIC CHANGE

↓

NEW SPECIES

SOLOMON ISLANDS

Nissan

Bougainville

Malaita

Vella Lavella

Rendova

San Cristobal

EVOLUTION STILL CONTINUES. Many geographic races are potentially new species in the making. Continued isolation of races of the golden whistler in the Solomon Islands all belonging to a single species, *Pachycephala pectoralis*, would probably convert them into reproductively isolated species.

MUTATIONS are important in the evolutionary process, even though so many in living populations seem to be harmful. In a population well-adapted to a particular environment, the most beneficial mutations have often already been incorporated. In addition, mutations with limited visible effects are known to be common.

Not all harmful traits are eliminated from the gene pool of a population. Selection is always a compromise. Even harmful characteristics may have some beneficial side effects (p. 93). Preservation of such genes provides a reservoir of potential change that may be of critical importance if environmental conditions change.

COLOR CHANGES IN MINK are the result of mutations.

ormal color

Pastel

Palomino

Sapphire

FACTORS ACCOUNTING FOR NEW SPECIES origin seem adequate to account also for all evolutionary change. Some writers refer to micro-evolution and macro-evolution, but these are not fundamentally different. Cumulative development of new species leads to what we later classify as new genera and higher groups.

Separation of descendants from ancestral populations by time reinforces geographic differences between contemporary races, as shown below.

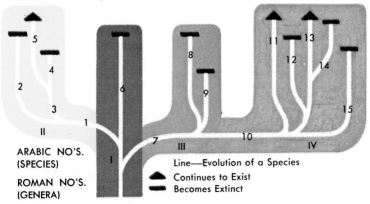

ARABIC NO'S. (SPECIES)

ROMAN NO'S. (GENERA)

Line—Evolution of a Species
Continues to Exist
Becomes Extinct

103

THE COURSE OF EVOLUTION

Pre-organic evolution that occurred before the appearance of life on earth left little direct evidence of the processes involved. Much smaller molecules were involved than in organic evolution, however, and the process resulted in bodies of much greater dimensions, such as stars and galaxies. The original material probably consisted of sub-atomic particles, such as neutrons, protons, and electrons, that later produced hydrogen. Much of the material in the visible universe seems to be hydrogen, which consists of a single proton. Heavier elements were probably produced from the lighter hydrogen by a process of neutron capture. Each neutron that was added yielded a new isotope.

The process by which hydrogen aggregated to form bodies such as stars, in which element-building took place, is still the subject of speculation. It may be a continuous process in which new hydrogen is being created constantly. Alternatively the apparent expansion of the universe may result from the "big bang" of a single episode of creation about 5 to 10 billion years ago. The universe might undergo pulsating movements, so that the present expansion would be followed by contraction. The "big bang" hypotheses tends to be the current favorite.

EARTH and the rest of the solar system probably originated by the aggregation of a cloud of cosmic dust. Earth's structures suggest that it formed from cold rather than from molten material.

THE PRIMITIVE EARTH on which life originated was an environment very different from any on earth today. Three lines of evidence suggest that the earth's primitive atmosphere probably consisted of hydrogen, helium, methane, and ammonia. The present atmosphere of nitrogen, carbon dioxide, and oxygen came later.

METEORITES appear to be material "left over" from the origin of the solar system. Analysis of their composition provides an indication of the possible "bulk composition" of the earth. Most meteorites are made of iron-nickel or "stony" material. A few (the carbonaceous chondrites) contain carbon compounds of extraterrestrial origin.

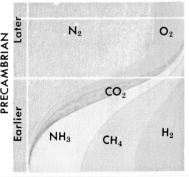

34-ton meteorite from Greenland

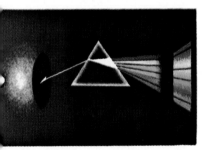

Dark lines in spectrum analysis are produced by absorption by cooler gas in front of glowing source.

SPECTROSCOPIC ANALYSIS of light from other planets shows that the six "basic" elements of living things are widely distributed. Hydrogen, oxygen, carbon, and nitrogen are among the most abundant elements in the solar system. Sulfur is ninth; phosphorous, sixteenth. This implies they were also probably present in the primitive earth.

THE ATMOSPHERES of planets most distant from the sun have probably changed the least. Their atmospheres include hydrogen, helium, methane (CH_4) and, in Jupiter and Saturn, ammonia (NH_3). Probable changes in the earth's atmosphere (water omitted) are based partly on analogy with these.

PALEOZOIC

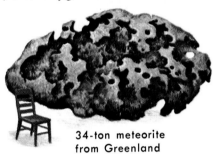

PRECAMBRIAN — Later / Earlier

N_2 O_2

CO_2

NH_3 CH_4 H_2

THE ORIGIN OF LIFE must have involved the development of proteins from their amino-acid components. An experiment by Stanley Miller and Harold Urey demonstrates one possible way in which this might have taken place on the primitive earth.

AMMONIA, methane, hydrogen, and steam were mixed together in a closed circulating system and then subjected to an electrical discharge. After several days the condensed water was found to contain a mixture of amino acids. The effects of lightning on the primitive atmosphere may have produced a similar non-biological synthesis of organic molecules.

Inorganic synthesis of other molecules, such as carbohydrates and nucleic acids, has also been demonstrated. These various compounds were probably preserved on the early earth by the absence of oxygen and of other living things.

ALL LIVING THINGS today depend, directly or indirectly, upon green plants for their food. The earliest organisms probably "fed" by some fermentation-like process upon the organic "broth" from which they arose, but this food source was limited. Changes in the earth's atmosphere caused both by solar radiation and by the effects of the earliest organisms produced an environment with increasing quantities of nitrogen and carbon dioxide. This probably encouraged the development of alternative feeding mechanisms, involving first the synthesis of more complex molecules. The more sophisticated process of photosynthesis in which sunlight supplies the energy for the conversion of atmospheric carbon dioxide into carbohydrates came later. Photosynthesis releases oxygen, so the early atmosphere underwent transformation from a reducing to an oxygenating environment.

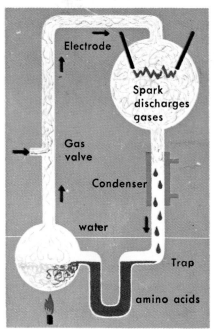

Electrode

Spark discharges gases

Gas valve

Condenser

water

Trap

amino acids

Miller-Urey apparatus, shown in diagrammatic form.

REPRODUCTION arose by duplication of large molecular aggregations by autocatalysis, in which electrically active compounds, such as proteins, could precipitate droplets of colloidal aggregates that were capable of developing into a surface membrane.

When increasing oxygen in the atmosphere reached a level to allow development of respiration, harmful ultraviolet solar radiation was increasingly filtered out as release of free oxygen produced a layer of atmospheric ozone. Colonization of surface waters, and later of the land, depended on the growing effectiveness of the ozone screen. The "sudden" appearance of hard-bodied invertebrate animals in Early Cambrian times may reflect the development of the ozone layer, which provided a protective environment.

EVOLUTION OF LIFE	billions of years before present	EVOLUTION OF EARTH'S ATMOSPHERE & HYDROSPHERE
	—0—	
*Earliest known fossil marine animals		Free oxygen sufficient for animal respiration
*Fossil green algae (multi-celled, sexual reproduction)	—1—	Free oxygen invades atmosphere; starts to form ozone layer which screens out ultraviolet rays. Weathering of rock begins
*Fossil bacteria and blue-green algae	—2—	
*Earliest known fossils (single-cell protists (bacteria) and simple plants (blue-green algae). Development of cell membrane	—3—	Free oxygen in hydrosphere increases; oxidizes iron

Development of photosynthesis; releases free oxygen to hydrosphere |
| Colloidal coacervates

Protein and macromolecules | | Fermentation (?); adds carbon dioxide to hydrosphere |
| Amino acids

Simplest compounds of C, H, O, and N | —4— | Primitive atmosphere probably H_2, H_2O, CH_4 and NH_3; no free oxygen. Intense ultraviolet radiation |

FORMATION OF PLANET EARTH

Critical events in the early history of living matter and in the development of atmosphere and hydrosphere. * denote fossils, the earlier part of the history being hypothetical (After Flint and others)

THE FOSSIL RECORD is the basis of our understanding of the history of life and the course of evolution. Fossils are the remains of or indications of prehistoric animals and plants preserved in the rocks of the earth's crust. Fossils are of many kinds and are formed by various processes, but the chances of any organism becoming fossilized are small. Thus, the fossil record is a very incomplete and rather biased record of the history of life. Recognition of this is important in interpreting the fossil record. Organisms lacking hard parts, for example, are rarely found as fossils. For this reason records of the early development of life are particularly meager.

WHOLE ANIMALS AND PLANTS are very rarely preserved in the fossil record. Woolly mammoths, up to 10 feet tall, found in Siberia and Alaska are examples of such preservation by a deep-freeze process.

AN OUTLINE of soft parts of organisms buried in fine mud is sometimes preserved as a carbon film, the more volatile components distilled off by heat and pressure in rocks. Examples are the trilobites and leaves.

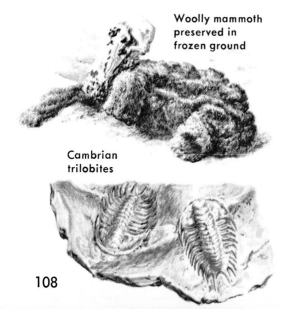

Woolly mammoth preserved in frozen ground

Cambrian trilobites

Fossil plant leaves from Pennsylvanian

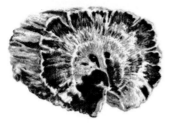

Growth rings are preserved in silica in petrified wood.

This clam shell is almost unaltered except for leaching.

MOST FOSSILS consist of only the hard parts of animals and plants, such as shells, bones, teeth, and wood. In a few cases these are almost unaltered, but usually they are leached and partly or wholly replaced by other minerals, especially silica (SiO_2) and calcite ($CaCO_3$). The replacing minerals may sometimes preserve the original microstructure, as in some silicified wood, but this is unusual.

Ammonite, calcium carbonate, replaced by pyrite (FeS_2).

IMPRESSIONS AND CASTS of animals and plants may be formed in porous rocks, such as sandstone, when all the original components are dissolved away. This leaves a cavity, which may later be filled by new minerals, carried in solution, to give a cast of the original outline.

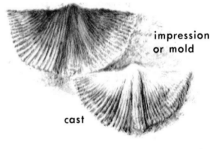

impression or mold

cast

BURROWS, TRAILS AND TRACKS may be preserved in sediments that are later consolidated into rocks.

Dinosaur tracks in sandstone

STONE ARTIFACTS are the most common remains of prehistoric man. They represent various types of tools and weapons.

Prehistoric hand axe

109

THE OLDEST FOSSILS found in rocks estimated to be about 2.7 billion years old, consist of simple plants, including lime-secreting algae, bacteria, and fungi. Various organic amino-acid residues are also known from these very ancient rocks. Well-preserved animal fossils first appear in rocks 600 million years old.

Microscopic colonies of algae from 1.6 billion years ago. Gunflint Formation, Ontario (x200)

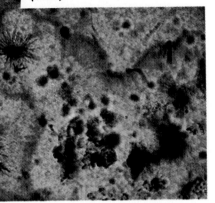

Precambrian Fossils

Segmented worm
Spriggina flounderi   1.5 in.
(After Glaessner)

Jellyfish
Medusian mawsoni
about 1 in.

(After Glaessner)

THE OLDEST PLANTS are preserved in cherts from North America, Africa, and Australia and range in age from 2 to about 3 billion years. They include filamentous and spherical algae and bacteria and other microscopic structures that are not easily classified. Some are closely similar to living forms. Other more widespread Precambrian fossils include optically active organic compounds of supposed organic origin.

Stromatolites, widely distributed in rocks of Precambrian age, are moundlike, laminated structures, a few feet in diameter, found in calcareous rocks. They represent the deposits of lime-secreting blue-green algae.

THE OLDEST ANIMALS are known from Ediacara, South Australia, in Precambrian rocks that lie only 500 feet below the Cambrian. They are soft-bodied animals, including jellyfish, segmented worms, sea pens, and some animals of unknown affinities. In contrast to the oldest plants, which are primitive, the oldest animals are relatively advanced types, suggesting a long earlier history.

Obolella, Lower Cambrian brachiopod. About 0.2 in.

Olenellus, a lower Cambrian trilobite. Length to 9 in.

The "sudden" appearance of fossil animals about 600 million years ago is one of the major evolutionary problems. It has been variously suggested that: (a) no Precambrian animals existed; (b) Precambrian animals did exist but lacked hard parts and were not fossilized; (c) Precambrian animal fossils have been destroyed by erosion and metamorphism; and (d) Precambrian animals were confined to isolated, oxygen-rich areas and are as yet undiscovered or unexposed as fossils.

None of these explanations is necessarily untrue. Early Cambrian diversification of animals extended over 30 million years, hence was not really "sudden." It seems probable that animals did not originate in late Precambrian times, that their earliest representatives were soft-bodied forms of restricted distribution, and that the later widespread appearance of hardbodied forms in Cambrian times may mark a response to some environmental change, such as the atmospheric composition or cut-off of ultraviolet radiation (p. 106). It was probably rapid because of the relative "emptiness" of many environments to animal life, and the strong selective pressure that the development of hard parts by any one group would exert on others.

111

Middle Cambrian sea based on specimens from Burgess Shale of British Columbia: (1) jellyfish, (2) sponge, (3) trilobite, (4) worm, (5) brachiopod, (6) xenopod arthropod

MARINE INVERTEBRATES were the most distinctive animals of Cambrian, Ordovician, and Silurian times— a period of some 200 million years. Although vertebrate fragments are found in Ordovician rocks, they were rare until Devonian times. The earliest invertebrates (p. 110) included jellyfish, sea pens, and segmented worms, but Cambrian faunas were dominated by trilobites, now extinct arthropods. Sponges, snails, echinoderms, and small horny bivalved brachiopods were abundant in shallow seas. In the Ordovician, corals, bryozoans (moss animals), and many new kinds of brachiopods and trilobites appeared. Protozoans were rare. Squidlike cephalopods, some 15 feet long, developed. In the Silurian, eurypterids, arthropods to 6 feet long, lived in deltas and estuaries.

Representatives of all the major living invertebrate phyla and nearly all the classes were established by Ordovician times. Since then, the major patterns of invertebrate life in the seas have changed little. A few major groups have become extinct, different geographic areas and different environments have supported different faunas, and genera and species have shown varied patterns of modification and extinction.

EARLY PALEOZOIC ANIMALS showed many adaptations to differing modes of life. They included fixed benthic forms, such as corals and brachiopods; vagrant benthic types, such as starfish and snails; free-swimming forms, such as cephalopods and eurypterids; and free-floating forms, such as jellyfish.

Comparable diversity existed in feeding habits. The phytoplankton, on which many living marine invertebrates feed, have siliceous and calcareous hard parts. These types are unknown in the Early Paleozoic, perhaps because their forerunners were soft-bodied. The hard parts of Early Paleozoic invertebrates are composed of various minerals. Cambrian forms consist chiefly of phosphatic, siliceous, and chitinous materials, but calcium carbonate became the predominant shell substance in Ordovician times. Little is yet known of the significance of this biochemical evolution. Original shell composition is often modified by subsequent alteration during fossilization (p. 108).

A Devonian coral reef: (1) trilobite, (2) cephalopod, (3) bryozoan, (4) brachiopod, (5) coral, (6) coral, (7) coral

THE OLDEST VERTEBRATES are fragments of armored fish found in rocks of Ordovician age in Wyoming and elsewhere. Fish remain rare as fossils until late Silurian times. They become diversified and abundant during the Devonian.

The origin of vertebrates is obscure. They belong to the Phylum Chordata, containing some members that lack a vertebral column (acorn worms, sea squirts, lancelets, and their kin) though they do have a supporting notochord and other features shared with the "higher" vertebrates. Larval acorn worms show striking similarities to larval echinoderms, suggesting that both groups may have arisen from a common but unknown ancestral stock.

AGNATHA, the most primitive group of fish, are represented today only by the hagfish and lampreys. Agnatha lack the true jaws and paired fins typical of most living fish.

Many of these oldest and most diversified of the early fish had a bony armor. Called ostracoderms ("bony skin"), they rarely exceeded a foot in length. They lived chiefly in streams and estuaries where presumably they fed on bottom muds or on suspended material. They are not known in rocks younger than the Devonian, perhaps because they were soft-bodied—like their living representatives.

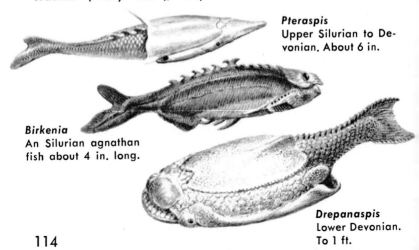

Pteraspis
Upper Silurian to Devonian. About 6 in.

Birkenia
An Silurian agnathan fish about 4 in. long.

Drepanaspis
Lower Devonian.
To 1 ft.

Climatius, Upper Silurian to Devonian, was a spiny acanthodian "shark" with rhomboid scales, 2 spines on back, and 5 pairs of ventral fins. Length 3 in.

Dunkleosteus was a jointed-necked marine arthrodire to 30 ft. long. It was the largest vertebrate of Devonian times.

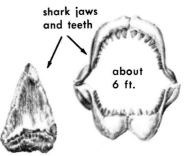

PLACODERMS (late Silurian to Permian) are the only vertebrate class to have become extinct. They reached their peak in the Devonian and are rare in younger Paleozoic rocks. Placoderms differ from Agnatha in having paired fins and primitive jaws, important features in later diversification of vertebrates.

Placoderms included both freshwater and marine forms, such as the 30-foot, jointed-necked arthrodires; small freshwater spiny acanthodians; and massively armored, strong-finned antiarchs.

Cladoselache, a shark from the Upper Devonian, with a streamlined naked body. To 4 ft.

shark jaws and teeth

about 6 ft.

Teeth of *Carcharodon,* a 40- to 50-foot shark from the Miocene

SHARKS AND RAYS belong to the Chondrichthyes, a class of predaceous, cartilaginous, open-gilled fish. Sharks show many adaptations to life in the open oceans, including streamlining, well-developed teeth, and spiny skin scales. Some living sharks reach a length of 50 feet. The earliest members of the group, which appeared in Devonian times, lived in fresh water.

Skates and rays, flattened for bottom-dwelling existence, have flattened teeth for crushing shells.

Loss of the bony armor, development of efficient jaw suspension, and more flexible fins provided both sharks and bony fish with an advantage over their placoderm ancestors. Isolated teeth and spines are the most common fossils.

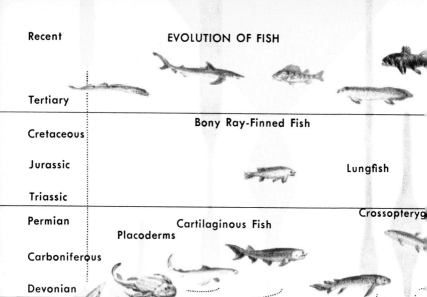

EVOLUTION OF FISH

Recent

Tertiary

Cretaceous

Jurassic

Triassic

Permian

Carboniferous

Devonian

Silurian

Ordovician

Bony Ray-Finned Fish

Lungfish

Crossopteryg

Cartilaginous Fish

Placoderms

Agnatha

BONY FISH (Osteichthyes) include nearly all living freshwater and marine species. They have strong, but flexible, bony skeletons and either scales or plates. Most kinds have an air bladder. Bony fish live in every kind of aquatic environment (even caves), and they outnumber all other vertebrates combined, both in numbers of species and of individuals. The oldest members were freshwater forms from the Middle Devonian. They include fish with two types of fins.

The ray-finned fish were a rare, freshwater group in the Paleozoic, but they became the dominant group in the Mesozoic and Cenozoic. Their scales became thinner, and their jaws and skeletons showed progressive improvement.

Cheirolepis, a Middle Devonian ray-finned fish. Length about 11 in.

Detail of ray fin, with typical supporting bones.

116

EVOLUTION OF AMPHIBIANS

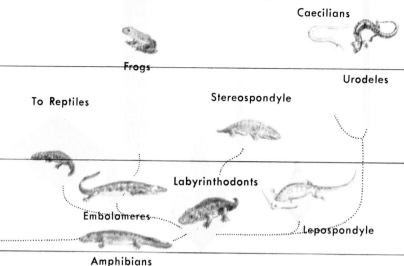

Caecilians

Frogs

Urodeles

To Reptiles

Stereospondyle

Labyrinthodonts

Embolomeres

Lepospondyle

Amphibians

AIR-BREATHING BONY FISH (Choanichthyes), a smaller group than the ray-finned fish, have internal nostrils that open into the mouth, as do those in land-living vertebrates. Living forms include the lungfish; three genera are known, one from each of the southern continents. They have powerful fins, supported not by a fan of slender bones as in the ray-finned fish but by a strong bony axis. They use these stout fins to "walk" from pool to pool during the dry season.

Lobefins, the other major group, includes the living marine coelacanths and their more generalized, freshwater, carnivorous, Devonian crossopterygian forebears. It was these that gave rise to the terrestrial vertebrates (pp. 94-95).

Osteolepis, from Middle Devonian, with thick, rhomboid scales and short, lobed fins. To 9 in.

lobe

fringe

Lobe fin, showing the strong supporting bones from which feet developed.

LIFE ON THE LAND was a comparatively late development. Life probably originated in the shallow seas, where the majority of invertebrate groups are still restricted. Life on the land involved major changes for these creatures that originated and lived in the oceans. The modifications included changes necessary for protection against drying up, new methods of support in air as opposed to the more buoyant water, breathing oxygen as opposed to extracting it from the water, new sources of food and water, and new reproductive mechanisms to assure fertilization in the absence of water. Colonization of rivers and lakes was only slightly less formidable, for it involved development of mechanisms to prevent dilution of body fluids

ARTHROPODS have exceeded all other groups in the diversity and number of their terrestrial and flying representatives. They gained a "flying start" by their tough, flexible outer covering and by their strong appendages. The oldest land arthropods are late Silurian millipedelike forms that may have been partly aquatic. Insects first appeared in the Devonian. By Carboniferous times, a variety of arthropods, including primitive winged insects, cockroaches, spiders, and scorpions, had appeared. Most groups arose in the Mesozoic.

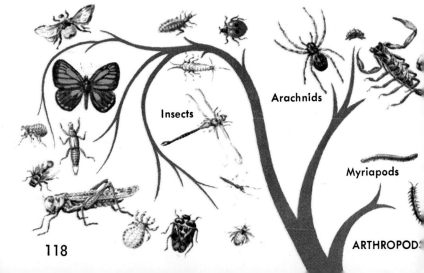

Insects

Arachnids

Myriapods

ARTHROPOD

that, in all animals, contain dissolved salts precisely adjusted to the osmotic balance of sea water.

Land dwelling, in spite of its problems, offered all the advantages of an empty environment. Because of the delicate interdependence of all living things, it is not surprising that both plants and animals seem to have colonized the land at about the same time during the Silurian and Devonian. The invasion of the land almost certainly involved the earlier invasion of fresh waters. Many living groups, which are essentially marine, contain a few freshwater colonists (clams and crustaceans, for example), but only the plants and three major groups of animals (snails, arthropods, and vertebrates) have become fully established on the land.

VERTEBRATES have established themselves on the land with varying degrees of success. Most amphibians are limited to areas near enough to water to allow them to return to it to reproduce. Most reptiles are restricted to areas from the tropical to the temperate zones. Mammals and birds are more widely distributed and adapted. Some vertebrates, including turtles and other extinct reptiles, porpoises, whales, and penguins, have undergone a secondary adaptation to marine life (p. 128).

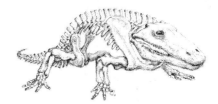

Skeleton of Permian amphibian, *Eryops*. Length about 5 feet.

SNAILS have invaded fresh waters and the land. Some have retained the protective shell, but others (slugs) are naked. Land forms move and feed by browsing, much like aquatic forms. They have developed lungs for breathing.

Land Snail, *Helix*

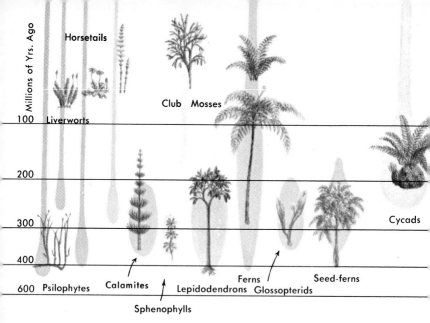

Millions of Yrs. Ago		
	Horsetails	
		Club Mosses
100	Liverworts	
200		
300		Cycads
400		
600	Psilophytes	Calamites

Ferns   Seed-ferns

Lepidodendrons Glossopterids

Sphenophylls

LAND PLANTS probably arose from green algae, which now exist in both the seas and in fresh waters. Like animals, different groups of plants show varying degrees of adaptation to land life.

BRYOPHYTES (mosses and liverworts) need water in reproduction and for protection from desiccation. Their partial adaptation to land life is analagous to that of the amphibians. Small plants, with leaves and stems, they lack woody tissues for support and circulation.

THALLOPHYTES, which includes the algae, fungi, and bacteria, lack the roots, stems, leaves, and vascular supporting and circulating system typical of higher plants. They are either unicellular or consist of loosely organized groups of cells. Limited to damp environments.

Club mosses are typical bryophytes.

The seaweed *Fucus* is a brown alga.

120

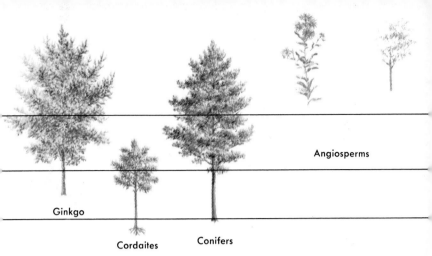

Ginkgo

Cordaites

Conifers

Angiosperms

VASCULAR PLANTS (Tracheophytes) include the majority of living plants. All have specialized vascular systems of conducting tissues that transport water and nutrients from the soil through the roots to the other parts of the plant. This system also provides support, allowing some of these plants to grow to great sizes. They also have an outer layer (cuticle) that prevents desiccation. The earliest vascular plants were seedless kinds, such as those shown in Devonian forest below.

Devonian forest scene. Shown are: (1) a primitive lycopod (*Protolepidodendron*), (2) tree fern (*Eospermatopteris*), and (3) scouring rush (*Calamophyton*). Psilopsids are low growing plants in foreground.

PSILOPSIDS, which include the earliest known vascular plants, lack roots. They have either primitive leaves or are leafless. Though widespread in Devonian times, they remained small in size. Only two genera survive.

SPHENOPSIDS include the living scouring rushes and similar Paleozoic plants that grew to 40 feet tall. They have roots and long, segmented, ribbed, cone-bearing stems with circlets of leaves at the nodes.

SEEDLESS VASCULAR PLANTS include psilopsids, lycopods, ferns, and sphenopsids. The adult plant produces spores that develop into small specialized leafless plants (gametophytes). These later produce gametes, or sex cells. Because sperm require water to reach the eggs, these seedless plants are restricted to damp environments. Widespread in the Paleozoic, they declined as seed-bearing plants expanded in Mesozoic.

LYCOPODS include the living club mosses and giant representatives from the Pennsylvanian coal forests.

FERNS, which still survive in large numbers, are spore-bearing plants. Some fossil and living forms grew to 50 feet tall.

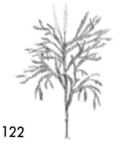

SEED-BEARING PLANTS are of two basic kinds: non-flowering and flowering. In the non-flowering groups (gymnosperms), the seed is not protected; it is "naked" —as in pine cones. In flowering plants (angiosperms), the seeds are protected. In both kinds, resistant pollen and eggs are produced directly from parent plants. Pollen fertilizes the egg, which develops into a seed which is protected from drying. As a result, seed-bearing plants have colonized a great variety of land areas and are the dominant living group of plants.

GYMNOSPERMS include (1) extinct *seed ferns*, perhaps ancestral to other groups; (2) *cycads* and their extinct relatives, which were abundant in the Mesozoic; (3) extinct *cordaites*, perhaps ancestral to conifers, (4) the living *ginkgos*; and (5) the widespread, abundant *conifers*.

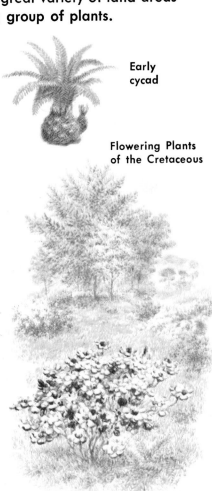

Early cycad

Flowering Plants of the Cretaceous

FLOWERING PLANTS (angiosperms) are represented today by over 250,000 species. They appeared in the Mesozoic and rapidly displaced the gymnosperms, which were then dominant. Their flowers are reproductive structures, many of them specially developed to attract insects that carry the male pollen to fertilize the female flowers. Enclosure of the seed in a protective covering also represents an advance over the gymnosperms. Flowering plants show numerous adaptations to different environments, ranging from desert cacti to tropical swamp trees and flowers. Changes in some animal groups appear related to changes in vegetation (p. 51 and 101).

AMPHIBIANS were the first terrestrial vertebrates, but they are only partly adapted to life on land. They need to return to water to lay their eggs, and their young develop in water. Most kinds are confined to damp environments as adults.

The oldest amphibians, the ichthyostegids from the Upper Devonian, arose from the crossopterygian lobe-finned fish, possibly in response to population pressure in the pools where the latter lived (p. 95). The stout bony axis and muscles of the fins and the presence of lungs adapted lobefins ideally for migration from stagnant and seasonal ponds. Life on the land provided unlimited oxygen supplies, the possibility of additional food sources, escape from predators, and the means of reaching other bodies of water.

LATE PALEOZOIC AMPHIBIANS showed great diversity. Their adaptive radiation onto land was rapid, and some forms underwent a secondary return to the water. Some labyrinthodonts were 15 feet in length. Amphibians dominated the land for over 100 million years. They declined in the early Mesozoic, perhaps as a result of competition with their better-adapted reptilian descendants. Living amphibians include newts, salamanders, frogs, toads, and caecilians.

Late Paleozoic coal-forming swamp with labyrinthodont amphibians.

Early reptiles differed from their amphibian ancestors in only minor ways. They underwent rapid diversification in Permian times.

THE RISE OF THE REPTILES marked a new stage of adaptation to life on land. Reptiles develop from an egg with a tough outer covering, providing a built-in food supply and a sealed, liquid-filled capsule for the developing embryo. The infant reptiles emerge from the egg more or less fully formed. Reptiles were thus able to colonize the land areas far removed from streams and lakes. Reptilian skin is scaly or cornified, a protection against drying up; the limbs and circulatory systems of reptiles are generally superior to those of amphibians. Reptiles underwent great diversification in Mesozoic times, dominating life not only on the land but also in the seas and in the air. Their decline, still not fully understood, was marked by the expansion of their descendants, the birds and mammals.

125

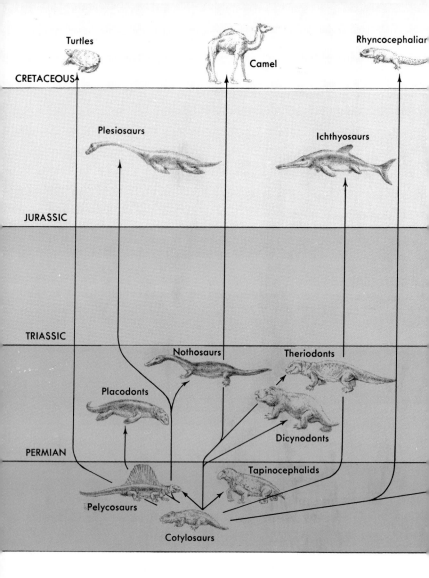

Turtles

Camel

Rhyncocephaliar

CRETACEOUS

Plesiosaurs

Ichthyosaurs

JURASSIC

TRIASSIC

Nothosaurs

Theriodonts

Placodonts

Dicynodonts

PERMIAN

Tapinocephalids

Pelycosaurs

Cotylosaurs

AQUATIC REPTILES were abundant in the Mesozoic, as reptiles mastered every major environment. Some were fishlike, others resembled the later seals, and still others were serpentlike.

FLYING REPTILES had light, strong skeleton and wings, supported by an elongated finger. Some were small; others had 20-foot wing spans. They were contemporaries, but not ancestors, of early birds.

126

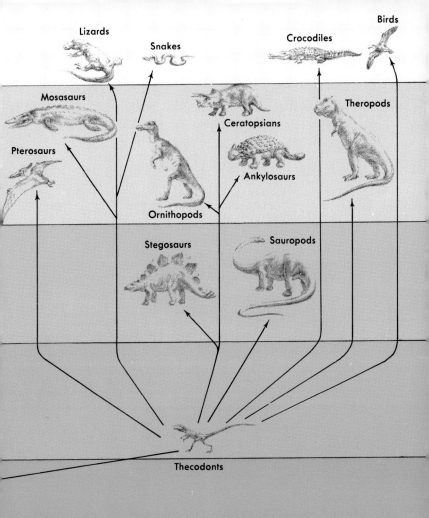

Birds

Lizards

Snakes

Crocodiles

Mosasaurs

Theropods

Ceratopsians

Pterosaurs

Ankylosaurs

Ornithopods

Stegosaurs

Sauropods

Thecodonts

The Dominance of the Reptiles (After Colbert)

DINOSAURS dominated land life for the 140 million years of the Mesozoic. Arising from thecodont ancestors, they included two groups with distinct hip structures: reptile-like saurischians and birdlike ornithischians. Worldwide in distribution, they were adapted to many different environments. They included herbivores and carnivores and also the largest, most heavily armored land animals that have ever lived. Reasons for their extinction in the late Mesozoic are obscure.

ADAPTIVE RADIATION of reptiles into forms adapted to life in different environments was paralleled by birds and mammals after the reptiles became extinct. Adaptive radiation occurs in the early history of many groups, usually followed by more specialized adaptations to niches within the wider environments.

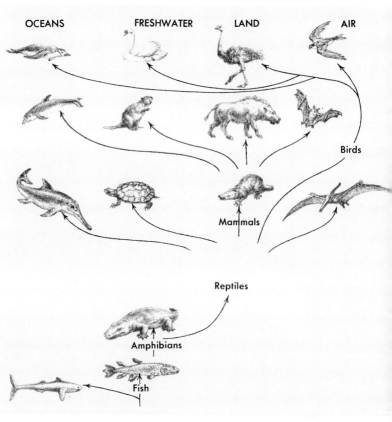

OCEANS   FRESHWATER   LAND   AIR

Birds

Mammals

Reptiles

Amphibians

Fish

EVOLUTIONARY CONVERGENCE in form between genetically unrelated penguins, dolphins, ichthyosaurs and sharks results from adaptation to similar environmental conditions. It is also present in many other groups. Although each of the mammalian tetrapod classes represents a new or distinctive adaption to life in various environments, the three "highest" classes have each successfully adapted to all environments.

Waterfowl

Hawks, Eagles, Vultures

Chickenlike Birds

Cranes, Rails, and Allies

Waders, Gulls, Auks

Herons, Flamingos

Doves, Parrots, Cuckoos

Pelicans

Ichthyornis

Diatryma

Archaeopteryx

Hesperornis

Owls and goatsuckers

enguins

Swifts and Hummingbirds

Loons

Climbing Birds and Rollers

Grebes

Ratites

Perching Birds

BIRDS are rare as fossils, because of their fragile skeletons and because many birds live in areas where burial conditions that lead to preservation are uncommon. Birds share the egg-laying characteristics of reptiles from which they arose, but the important, distinctive features in their diversification and survival are their superb adaptation to flying, their care of the young, their feather covering, and their warm-bloodedness. The history of some important groups of birds is shown above.

EVOLUTION OF MAMMALS (Triassic to Recent) from the mammal-like therapsid reptiles (p. 124) is well documented in the fossil record. Some fossils are so transitional in character between the two groups that there is doubt which they represent. Mammals are typically covered with hair or fur, have differentiated teeth, are warm-blooded, and have highly developed senses. Nearly all mammals give birth to their young only after a long period of protective embryonic development within the mother's body, and then the mother feeds the young milk secreted from her mammary glands. These features and the highly developed brains of most mammals must have been of major importance in the evolutionary success of the group. Mammals' regulated body temperature enable them to survive in a much greater environmental range than did the reptiles.

THE OLDEST MAMMALS were shrew-sized creatures, a few of which reached about one foot in length. They are known from their tiny fossil bones. These mammals remained inconspicuous throughout the Mesozoic.

Ancestral fossil mammal

MONOTREMES, like the echidna (spiny anteater) and platypus (p. 53), lay eggs and secrete milk from modified sweat glands. Their primitive reptilian characteristics suggest that they are an ancient group, and they are limited to the Australia area.

Echidna

Platypus

nursing young

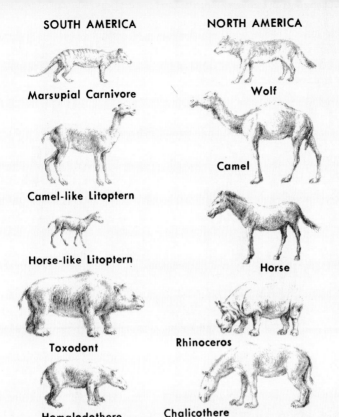

SOUTH AMERICA | NORTH AMERICA

Marsupial Carnivore

Wolf

Camel-like Litoptern

Camel

Horse-like Litoptern

Horse

Toxodont

Rhinoceros

Homalodothere

Chalicothere

MARSUPIAL MAMMALS (Cretaceous to Recent), such as kangaroos and opossums, give birth to very immature young that are sheltered and fed inside their mother's pouch. Marsupials were widespread in South America in the Cenozoic, showing many examples of convergence (p. 128) with placental mammals as illustrated above.

The joining of North and South America by the emergence of the Isthmus of Panama in the late Cenozoic ended the isolation in which these marsupials had developed. Competition with the better adapted North American placentals resulted in the extinction of most marsupials. Many have survived in Australia because of that continent's continuing isolation. (After Simpson)

PLACENTAL MAMMALS include most living mammals. Because the embryo is nourished and sustained by the placenta within the mother's womb, the newborn are more mature than are marsupials, presumably an important evolutionary advantage. The oldest (Cretaceous) were shrewlike insectivores.

131

EARLY CENOZOIC MAMMALS showed a period of explosive radiation, replacing the Mesozoic ruling reptiles in almost every environment. Reconstruction above of scene some 50 million years ago included ancestral lemur *Notharctos* (1), carnivores *Oxyaena* (2), *Mesonyx* (3), hoofed mammals *Palaeosyops* (4), a titanothere (5), and the amblyods *Eobasileus* (6), *Uintatherium* (7), and *Coryphodon* (8).

Phenacodus

ARCHAIC HERBIVOROUS, HOOFED MAMMALS included *Phenacodus*, an advanced condylarth, with a long tail, five toes, and a carnivorelike skull. Contemporaries were amblypods and uintatheres (above), with teeth modified for chewing vegetation. The clawed toes of ancestral forms later became modified to hooves.

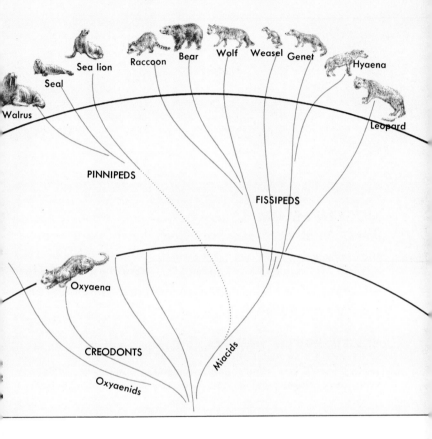

EVOLUTION OF CARNIVORES (After Colbert)

Walrus • Seal • Sea lion • Raccoon • Bear • Wolf • Weasel • Genet • Hyaena • Leopard

PINNIPEDS

FISSIPEDS

Oxyaena

CREODONTS

Oxyaenids

Miacids

ARCHAIC CARNIVOROUS MAMMALS—the creodonts—were mostly small, slender, long-tailed creatures. They developed claws, sharp teeth, and supple limbs. Some reached the size of lions. Most creodonts became extinct in the Eocene. From weasel-like members of this group there subsequently developed the ancestors of living cats, dogs, and bears.

LATER CARNIVORES included ancestral forms of fissiped (split-footed) cats, dogs, hyenas, and weasels, all of which appeared at different times. Web-footed carnivores (seals, walruses) invaded the oceans in Miocene times. The closely related cetaceans, including dolphins and whales, appeared in the Eocene and are superbly adapted to marine life.

133

MODERN MAMMALS arose in Eocene and Oligocene times. Pleistocene reconstruction shows giant ground sloth *Megatherium* (1), bison (2), saber-tooth cat (3), horses (4), woolly mammoth (5), camel-like *Camelops* (6), glyptodont (7), a huge beaver *Castoroides* (8), and ground sloth *Mylodon* (9).

MODERN HOOFED MAMMALS (Ungulates) include odd-toed horses, tapirs, and rhinos, and even-toed, cloven-hoofed cattle, pigs, camels, and deer, which displaced the earlier odd-toed ungulates. Changes in vegetation had an effect.

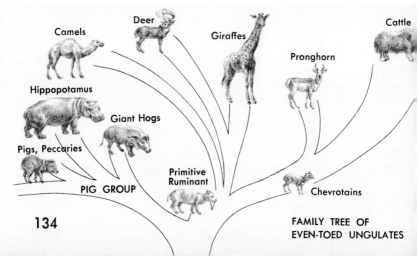

FAMILY TREE OF EVEN-TOED UNGULATES

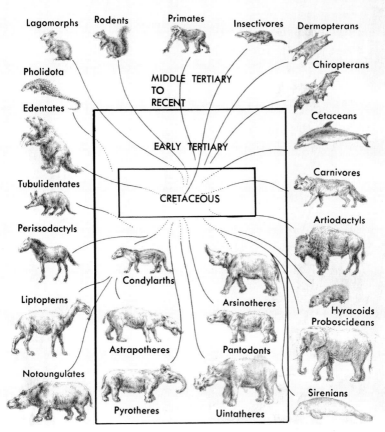

Lagomorphs
Rodents
Primates
Insectivores
Dermopterans
Pholidota
Chiropterans
Edentates
MIDDLE TERTIARY TO RECENT
Cetaceans
EARLY TERTIARY
Carnivores
Tubulidentates
CRETACEOUS
Artiodactyls
Perissodactyls
Condylarths
Arsinotheres
Liptopterns
Hyracoids Proboscideans
Astrapotheres
Pantodonts
Notoungulates
Sirenians
Pyrotheres
Uintatheres

Adaptive radiation of placental mammals. (After Colbert.)

Radiation of mammals into every environment is typified by their mastery of the air and the oceans as well as the land. Bats and ancestral whales both appeared in the early Tertiary. On the land, specialized mammalian groups developed. Rodents and rabbits adapted to a variety of foods and ways of life, including burrowing. Primates, many adapted to life in the trees, arose early in the Tertiary. Elephants and edentates (sloths and armadillos) represent further specialization in adaptations.

135

EVIDENCE OF EVOLUTION of one species into another over geologic time is provided by many mammalian groups. Two typical examples are given here.

TITANOTHERES were a group of large Tertiary mammals. Their evolutionary development is shown in historical sequence below. Other forms also existed, and their evolution is also well documented. (After Osborn.)

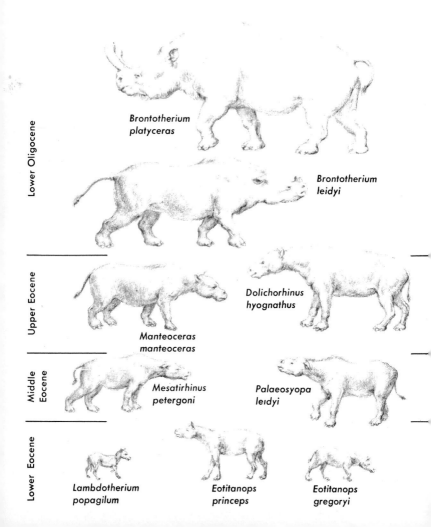

Lower Oligocene

Brontotherium platyceras

Brontotherium leidyi

Upper Eocene

Manteoceras manteoceras

Dolichorhinus hyognathus

Middle Eocene

Mesatirhinus petergoni

Palaeosyopa leidyi

Lower Eocene

Lambdotherium popagilum

Eotitanops princeps

Eotitanops gregoryi

EVOLUTION OF PROBOSCIDEANS, GREATLY SIMPLIFIED.
(AFTER OSBORN.)

Elephas
Pleist.-Rec.

Loxodonta
Pleist.-Rec.

Mammuthus
Pleist.

Stegodon
Plio.-Pleist.

Gnathobelodon
Plio.

Platybelodon
Mio.-Plio.

Amebelodon
Mio.-Plio.

Mammut
Mio.-Plio.

Moeritherium
Eoc.-Olig.

Palaeomastodon
Olig.

Gomphotherium
Mio.-Plio.

137

GEOGRAPHIC DISTRIBUTION of living mammals reflects the pattern of interconnection between continents during the geologic past.

EUROPE, ASIA, AND NORTH AMERICA were connected for much of Cenozoic time, allowing migration and explaining many similarities of their present faunas. The differences that do exist reflect differing climatic environments and recent development of desert and mountain barriers to migration.

The faunas of South America, Australia, and Africa south of the Sahara are quite distinct. These continents have been separated from one another throughout the Cenozoic. North African mammals are more similar to those of Europe.

Bison

Reindeer

Wild Horse

Hedgehog

PLAEARCTIC

Marco Polo Sheep

ORIENTAL

Indian Elephant

Polecat

Tiger

Tapir

Aardvark

Gibbon

Bin

Water Buffalo

ETHIOPIAN

Gorilla

Flying Phalanger

African Elephant

Bandicoot

Wombat

Native

Gnu

Zebra

Giraffe

Koala

Kangaroo

AUSTRALIAN

ISOLATION of South America and Australia produced very different mammalian faunas, in which marsupials were at first the dominant forms. They remain abundant in Australia because of its continuing isolation. Interconnection of North and South America in the late Tertiary led to competition and extinction of many South American placentals.

Convergent evolution in external form between North American placental mammals and fossil South American marsupials (p. 131) demonstrates the influence of natural selection in adaptation to similar modes of life.

Geographic distribution of other animal groups does not necessarily show same boundaries as mammals. Plants and marine invertebrates, for example, have quite different dispersal means, and therefore different distribution patterns.

Caribon

Mountain Goat

Musk Ox

Bison

NEARCTIC

Porcupine

Pronghorn Antelope

Howler Monkey

Kinkajou

NEOTROPICAL

Anteater

Sloth

Capybara

Tapir

139

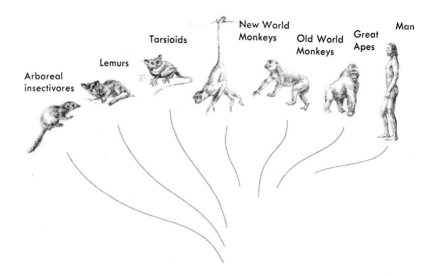

Relationships between the main groups of primates. (After Colbert.)

PRIMATES are the mammalian order to which lemurs, tarsiers, monkeys, apes, and man belong. They tend to be rather rare as fossils, largely because of their characteristically arboreal habits. Most primates show two fundamental adaptations to their tree-dwelling existence: stereoscopic vision and hands capable of grasping. These two features, present in all but the most primitive members, allow the primates to judge distances accurately and to swing from branch to branch. They were also important, together with his large brain, in the development of ground-dwelling man, allowing him to develop increasing skills in making and using tools.

140

PROSIMIANS (pre-monkeys) include living lemurs, aye-ayes, bushbabies, and the more monkey-like tarsioids. They arose in the Paleocene, probably from arboreal insectivores, and became diversified during the early Tertiary. They declined in numbers during late Tertiary times, probably because of competition from their descendants, the anthropoids. Prosimians still survive in such places as Madagascar and Southeast Asia. Prosimians have less well-developed binocular vision and grasping limbs than other primates.

Notharctos, an Eocene prosimian, about 18 inches high.

ANTHROPOIDS include monkeys, apes, and men. They developed in the Oligocene and Miocene from primitive prosimian ancestors. Old World monkeys show fundamental differences from those of the New World. Flat-nosed, prehensile-tailed South American forms, such as marmosets, capuchins, and spider monkeys, seem to be more primitive. Old World and New World monkeys arose independently from prosimians. Their similarities are the result of convergent evolution.

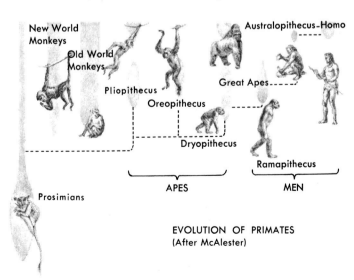

EVOLUTION OF PRIMATES
(After McAlester)

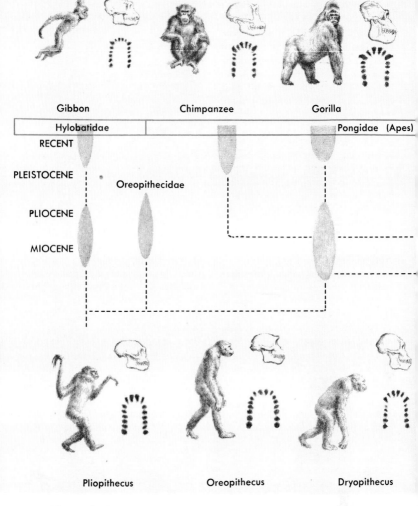

Gibbon Chimpanzee Gorilla

Hylobatidae Pongidae (Apes)

RECENT

PLEISTOCENE

Oreopithecidae

PLIOCENE

MIOCENE

Pliopithecus Oreopithecus Dryopithecus

HOMINOIDS—apes and men—are classified together in a single superfamily, Hominoidea. They show fewer differences from one another than do the Old World from the New World monkeys, which are in separate superfamilies. The history of the hominoids above shows their possible evolutionary relationships as revealed by skulls and by dental patterns.

142

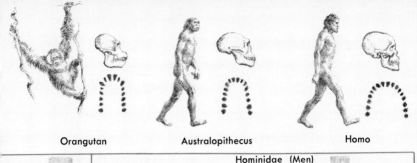

| Orangutan | Australopithecus | Homo |

Hominidae (Men)

Ramapithecus

?

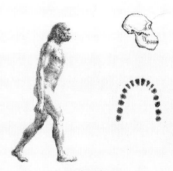

Ramapithecus

Australopithecus

LIVING APES include the chimpanzee and gorilla, which are chiefly ground-living forms, and the gibbon and the orangutan, which are beautifully adapted to arboreal life. All lack the typical tail of monkeys. All, except perhaps the gibbons, seem to have arisen from generalized apes that were widespread in the Old World in Miocene and Pliocene times. *Dryopithecus (Proconsul)*, which included several forms most probably of apelike proportions, may also have given rise to the ancestors of man. (Illustrations adapted from many authors.)

143

THE FAMILY OF MAN which spans the last 2 million years, includes three genera. Two of them are now extinct. Because of the rarity of primate fossils and perhaps also because of the intense interest in the origin of man, there is some disagreement concerning the detailed relationships of particular species within the broad pattern of evolutionary development. New discoveries are still being made, and the provisional account given here may well require later modification.

RAMAPITHECUS, a still poorly known hominid, has been found in late Miocene and Pliocene rocks of India and Africa. The pattern of its teeth shows a rather smooth semicircular outline, which is far more similar to that of living man than to the quadrate pattern of the apes (p. 142). Little is known about other parts of the skeleton, and because of this, the reconstruction shown below is very tentative. But the tooth pattern is so "humanistic" that it seems probable that *Ramapithecus* was closely related to modern man.

AUSTRALOPITHECUS (Southern-ape) is also regarded as closely related to modern man, probably directly ancestral to the **genus** *Homo* to which we assign our own species, *Homo sapiens.*

Australopithecines, once widespread in Africa, are now thought to include two species (p. 143). They were ground dwellers about 4 feet tall. Already, however, they had an upright posture. Bones found with their remains suggest that they were carnivores, but this is not certain. In dental pattern and in general skull form, they were very manlike, despite their rather protruding jaws and brow ridges. Their brain capacity (about 600 cc) was only half that of modern man.

There is still some doubt whether crudely chipped stone tools associated with fossil deposits were made and used by australopithecines or by their descendants and ultimate contemporaries, *Homo erectus.* Australopithecines became extinct about half a million years ago. Recent discoveries in Kenya suggest that early forms may date back as far as 2.6 million years.

WHAT IS MAN? This question is surprisingly difficult to answer when applied to fossils. It seems better to restrict the term "man" to our own species, *Homo sapiens,* and to regard other closely related forms as prehuman, though some of these manlike creatures did share the human characteristic of tool manufacture. Modern man appeared about 500,000 years ago.

HOMO ERECTUS is known from fossils found in the Pleistocene sediments ranging from about 750,000 to 200,000 years in age. Though sometimes described by other names (most commonly *Pithecanthropus*), individuals of the species are known from Java, China, Africa, and Asia. *H. erectus* was an erect, ground-dwelling individual who fashioned various tools and was apparently a hunter. Manlike in structure and in appearance, *H. erectus* had a brain capacity of 900-1100 cc, intermediate between that of *Australopithecus* and modern man. *H. erectus* was a contemporary and perhaps a competitor of later australopithecines from whose earlier members "he" evolved. *H. erectus* used fire and led a communal life.

MODERN MAN, *Homo sapiens,* seems to have arisen from *H. erectus.* For almost 200,000 years, the two species were contemporaries. Modern man is characterized by less conspicuous brows and jaws than the earlier hominids and had a much larger brain (av. capacity about 1350 cc).

Several races were involved in the fossil history of man. Neanderthal man, long regarded as a distinct species, was a race of heavy-browed, muscular individuals. The later Cro-Magnon race had facial features that more closely resembled those of modern man. Although these differences are real, they seem analogous only to those of living human races, between which interbreeding frequently takes place.

Neanderthal Man

NEANDERTHAL MAN, now regarded as a race of our own species, lived throughout Europe, the Mediterranean area, and parts of Asia Minor from about 110,000 to 35,000 years ago, a period that included three episodes of glaciation. Neanderthal men lived in caves and were skillful toolmakers and hunters. They were not the stupid brutes they are often pictured as being.

Cro-Magnon Man

CRO-MAGNON MAN replaced Neanderthal Man in Europe about 35,000 years ago, probably migrating from the Middle East. Physically similar to modern man, Cro-Magnon man manufactured superior tools and produced masterpieces of art and sculpture (p. 149).

THE EVOLUTION OF TOOLS. Weapons, societies, and cultures arise from and reflect man's physical and mental evolution. Binocular vision, manual dexterity, and increasing mental capacity were paralleled by the increasing perfection of man's work as a craftsman.

THE OLDEST TOOLS were probably used but not made, consisting of stones and boulders conveniently shaped by nature. Later tools were crudely chipped and shaped axes and scrapers. These were gradually supplemented and replaced by delicately chipped blades and arrowheads of a variety of materials, including bone.

About 10,000 years ago, the early culture of chipped implements, the Paleolithic, gave way in Europe to the Neolithic, which was marked by finely ground and polished tools and weapons. About 5,000 years ago, man first learned to fashion implements of metal. The "stone age" still persists among some living peoples.

PEBBLE TOOL
Abbevillian

SCRAPER
Mousterian

HAND AXES
Acheulian

POINT
Mousterian

SPOKESHAVE
Aurignacian

BONE AND ANTLER WEAPONS
Magdelinian

WEAPON HEADS
Solutrean

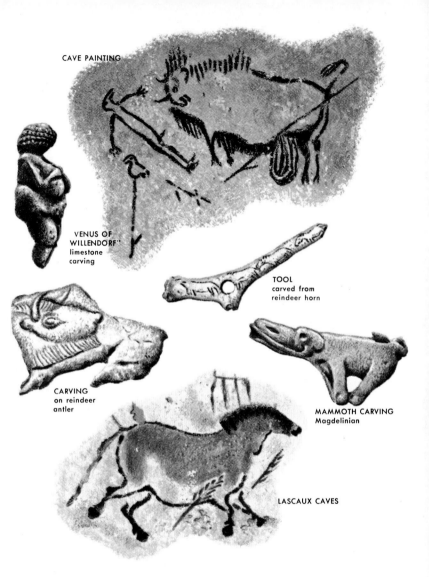

CAVE PAINTING

VENUS OF WILLENDORF" limestone carving

TOOL carved from reindeer horn

CARVING on reindeer antler

MAMMOTH CARVING Magdelinian

LASCAUX CAVES

CULTURAL EVOLUTION of man is glimpsed in cave paintings and carvings that date to about 28,000 years ago. Both are chiefly depictions of hunting and fertility. They may have had "magical" significance.

Man's ancient belief in survival after death is shown by Neanderthal and Cro-Magnon skeletons buried in fetal or sleeping positions, with implements and tokens to be used in the new life.

EVOLUTION OF HUMAN SOCIETIES arose from man's growing adaptation to his environment. Such landmarks as the discovery and use of fire by *Homo erectus* and the development of crop cultivation, animal husbandry, and pottery by Neolithic men produced radical changes in the patterns of human life. Man, originally a nomadic hunter and herbivore, could then construct dwellings and gather into groups who established settlements.

The need for communication fostered the development of increasingly sophisticated language. The growing size of communities necessitated the division of the various tasks involved in survival and the creation of some form of government. We know little of the detailed development of any of these, for writing was not invented until about 5,000 years ago. Early recorded history is very patchy, being infinitely more complete for some parts of the world, such as Egypt, than for others. The earliest societies and their unwritten languages, unlike the implements of early man, left no records in the stone.

THE MEANING OF EVOLUTION

Even before Darwin published *The Origin of Species*, some religious leaders attacked the concept of evolution because they thought it threatened their viewpoint; others have embraced it as a new insight into the work of God in the created world. Evolutionary theorists have claimed evolution as a justification for militant political tactics; others have endorsed it as illustrating the inevitability of harmonious political development. Some economists have claimed it as an argument for *laissez-faire* economic policies, while a few scientists have used it as a basis for a new code of ethics. Some popular writers, attacking traditional religious belief, have adopted evolutionism as a new religion. Seldom has a scientific theory so quickly become all things to all men. Seldom has a natural process been so carelessly used as an expository basis for the whole pattern of human life.

Contemporary cartoon and verse indicates Victorian interest in the meaning of evolution.

> Am I Satyr or Man?
> Pray tell me who can,
> And settle my place in the scale,
> A man in ape's shape,
> An anthropoid ape,
> Or monkey deprived of his tail?
> The *Vestiges* taught,
> That all came from naught
> By "development," so called,
> "progressive;"
> That insects and worms
> Assume higher forms
> By modification excessive,
> Then DARWIN set forth,
> In a book of much worth
> The importance of "Nature's selection;"
> . . . .

MONKEYANA.

Victorian cartoon depicts a puzzled Darwin and his ancestors.

The Implications of Evolution

The process of evolution is a fact. Numerous lines of evidence indicate the descent of new species by modification of ancestral forms over extended periods. Although the mechanism is still theoretical, there is very strong evidence that natural selection, genetic variation, and isolation are the chief components. (p. 102)

Evolution, like any other natural process or scientific theory, is theologically neutral. It describes mechanisms, but not meaning. It is based upon the recognition of order but incorporates no conclusion concerning the origin of that order as either purposeful or purposeless.

Although evolution involves the interpretation of natural events by natural processes, it neither assumes nor provides particular conclusions concerning the ultimate sources or the significance of materials, events or processes.

Evolution provides no obvious conclusions concerning political or economic systems. Evolution no more supports evolutionary politics (whatever they might be) than does the Second Law of Thermodynamics support political disorder or economic chaos.

Evolution offers no basis for ethics. It is not self-evident that survival is the highest good and that any means of its attainment is virtuous. T.H. Huxley wrote "The ethical progress of society depends, not on imitating the comic process, still less in running away from it, but in combating it."

EVOLUTION PROVIDES A PERSPECTIVE for man, hence is a significant contribution to human understanding. Recognition of the immensity of the span of geologic time, the awesome scale of cosmic dimensions and processes involved in the long period of pre-organic evolution, and the place of man himself within the endless diversity of the teeming life on the frail surface of our planet—all these help to enlighten and sustain man as he faces the challenge, the dilemma, and the mystery of his human condition.

Mankind, the product of organic evolution, is now technically equipped with power, if not the will, to control the future development of life on earth. Psychosocial evolution has now displaced the older processes of organic evolution in human communities. Knowledge, traditions, values, and skills are now transmitted from one generation to another through books and teaching institutions rather than being learned anew "from scratch" by each new individual.

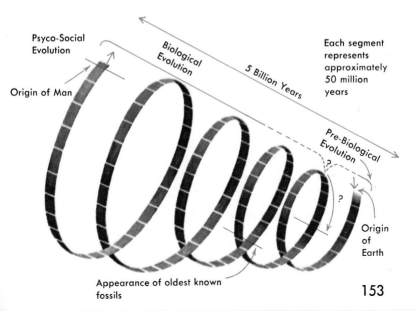

Psyco-Social Evolution

Origin of Man

Biological Evolution

5 Billion Years

Each segment represents approximately 50 million years

Pre-Biological Evolution

Origin of Earth

Appearance of oldest known fossils

153

THE FUTURE EVOLUTION OF MAN, of other species, and perhaps of the whole intricate ecosystem of which we are a part now stands in jeopardy. The pollution of the atmosphere on which our existence depends has now reached a crisis of major proportions in most industrialized areas of the world. Rapidly dwindling reserves of such essential commodities as petroleum and many metals threaten the future not only of industrial production but also of technologically based society. A continuing explosion of human population, especially in the less industrialized areas of the world, raises the awesome possibility of widespread famine and starvation within the next 30 years.

Man already possesses the technical power to solve these three major problems: pollution, dwindling mineral resources, and overpopulation. Whether he has the wisdom, the will, and the energy to solve them remains to be seen. It is ironic that the future of the age-long process of organic evolution may now depend on the conscious choice of man, a product of that process. The danger, the challenge, and the choice involve mankind in a common peril and a common hope.

Evolution provides no easy answers to man's long search for meaning and no instant solutions to man's most pressing problems. It is rather for man himself now to provide the input—in the recognition of an ethic beyond that of survival, of a purpose beyond that of gain, and of a vision of life beyond that of mechanism and process. On such collective commitments of men and of nations depend the survival of mankind and the future course of evolution.

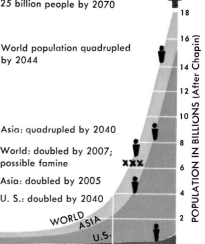

Pollution of atmosphere in industrial areas is a worldwide problem. World famine poses an increasingly severe threat as burgeoning population competes for limited resources. World population projections suggest global population of 25 billion by 2070.

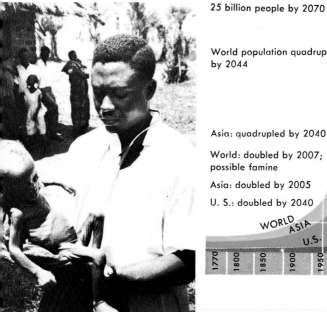

25 billion people by 2070

World population quadrupled by 2044

Asia: quadrupled by 2040

World: doubled by 2007; possible famine

Asia: doubled by 2005

U. S.: doubled by 2040

WORLD
ASIA
U.S.

1770 1800 1850 1900 1950 1970 2000 2050

POPULATION IN BILLIONS (After Chapin)

0 2 4 6 8 10 12 14 16 18

MORE INFORMATION

The following list of books is only an introduction to the voluminous literature on evolution. Many museums also provide displays, talks, and literature.

Historical

Darwin, Charles, *The Origin of Species,* Oxford University Press, N.Y., 1956. (6th ed., 1872 reprinted: The World Classics.)

Greene, J. C., *Darwin and the Modern World View,* Mentor Books, N.Y., 1963.

Moorehead, A., *Darwin and the Beagle,* Harper and Row, N.Y. 1969.

The Process of Evolution

DeBeer, G., *Atlas of Evolution,* Nelson and Sons, London, 1964.

Mayr, E., *Animal Species and Evolution,* Oxford University Press, N.Y. 1963.

Moore, R., *Evolution,* Time-Life, Inc., N.Y., 1962.

Savage, J. M., *Evolution,* Holt, Rinehart and Winston, N.Y., 1963.

Sheppard, P. M., *Natural Selection and Heredity,* Hutchinson, London, 1958.

Simpson, G. G., *The Major Features of Evolution,* Columbia University Press, N.Y., 1953.

Smith, J. M., *The Theory of Evolution,* Penguin Books, Harmondsworth, 1958.

Tax, S., *Evolution after Darwin,* University of Chicago Press, Chicago, 1960.

The Course of Evolution

Colbert, E. H., *Evolution of the Vertebrates,* John Wiley, N.Y., 1955.

Rhodes, F. H. T., *The Evolution of Life,* Penguin Books, Baltimore, 1974.

Rhodes, F. H. T., H. S. Zim, and F. R. Shaffer, *Fossils, a Guide to Prehistoric Life,* Golden Press, N.Y., 1963.

The Evolution of Man

Dobzhansky, T., *Mankind Evolving,* Yale University Press, New Haven, 1962.

Howell, F. Clark, *Early Man,* Time-Life Books, N.Y., 1965.

LeGros Clark, W. E., *History of the Primates,* British Museum of Natural History, London, 1954; *The Fossil Evidence of Human Evolution,* University of Chicago Press, Chicago, 1964.

Oakley, K. P., *Man the Tool-Maker,* British Museum of Natural History, London, 1963.

The Meaning of Evolution

Barbour, I. G., *Issues in Science and Religion,* SCM Ltd., London, 1966.

Lack, D., *Evolutionary Theory and Christian Belief; the Unresolved Conflict,* Methuen and Co., Ltd., London, 1957.

Simpson, G. G., *The Meaning of Evolution,* Mentor Books, N.Y., 1951.

Teilhard de Chardin, P., *The Phenomenon of Man,* Harper and Brothers, N.Y., 1959.

INDEX

157